Welcome to the Neighborhood!

Cooper's Ferry Development Association, master

developer of the Camden Waterfront, welcomes the

Battleship New Jersey as the newest attraction on

the Camden Waterfront, joining the New Jersey

State Aquarium, Tweeter Center, Camden

Riversharks baseball club and Campbell's Field,

Camden Children's Garden, Wiggins Park and the

South Jersey Performing Arts Center in

providing an exceptional brand of entertainment,

education and family fun.

COOPER'S FERRY
DEVELOPMENT ASSOCIATION, INC.

C A M D E N
WATERFRONT

    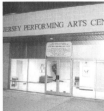 

To Shelby,

I know one day you will be able to read this. Enjoy and visit the ship often to keep her legacy alive.

Best Regards,

Carol Comegno

Signed on board the battleship

Dec. 16, 2003

The battleship USS New Jersey
From birth to berth

Carol Comegno · Courier-Post

ACKNOWLEDGMENTS

The *Courier-Post* wishes to thank these organizations and people for their help in compiling this book:

The Home Port Alliance

David B. McGuigan, Captain, United States Navy (Ret.)

Robert Elliott, Lt. Commander, United States Navy (Ret.)

Vincent Falso, Commissaryman 2nd Class, United States Navy (Ret.), president of the Battleship New Jersey Museum Society

Dozens of former shipyard workers and *USS New Jersey* crew members

Author
Carol Comegno

A senior *Courier-Post* reporter, Comegno covered the quest to bring the battleship to Camden, New Jersey. She was aboard for part of its last Panama Canal transit and documented its arrival home and restoration as a museum.

Editors
Larry Rosenthal, Laurie Stuart

Art director
Jeffrey L. Dauber

Photo editor
Bob Ringham

Photographers
Scott Anderson, Paris L. Gray, Ron Karafin, Chris LaChall, Tina Markoe Kinslow, Jose Moreno, Clark Perks, Al Schell, Avi Steinhardt, Shawn Sullivan, John Ziomek

Photo production
Lorraine Agnew

Graphics
Sheldon Sneed

President and publisher
Dan A. Martin

Executive editor
William C. Hidlay

Managing editor
Stuart Shinske

Marketing development
Carl Lovern Jr.

Gannett New Jersey Trenton bureau chief
Robert E. Ingle

The 600-pound ship's bell of the *USS New Jersey* waits to be rung as sailors line up on the bow of the battleship. The bell was used for ceremonial functions and to mark time. Removed at the ship's final decommissioning in 1991, it was being reinstalled on the *New Jersey* after restoration.
Courtesy of the Home Port Alliance

Cover photograph:
Twilight of an era – gunnery practice at dusk, 1980s.

Preceding page:
Multiple targeting capabilities, 1987.

Back cover photograph:
Opening day for the public, October 15, 2001.

Videos of the battleship, stories dating to 1939 and future stories about the ship are available on the *Courier-Post* Web site, www.courierpostonline.com

FOREWORD

"She's one hell of a foxhole."

That's what this old infantry veteran had in his mind as he walked the broad main deck of the *USS New Jersey* on a warm October evening in 2001, the gleaming skyline of Philadelphia shining in the background, the smoke from the destroyed World Trade Center still drifting in the dusky sky above Manhattan less than 100 miles to the north.

This foxhole is steel, and even though the signs of time can be traced in the many welds around her passageways and in the gashes in the teak planking on her decks, her mighty strength embraces you like a loving, assuring mother. And you take warm comfort from her presence.

How could any enemy not be cowed by the huge guns that thrust out from her girth, probing for those who would mock liberty and the United States of America? How could any person tired, poor, yearning to be free, not take solace from this symbol of power and freedom?

She graces the shoreline of the Delaware River in Camden, New Jersey, as she graced the seas of the Pacific, Atlantic, the Persian Gulf, the waters off Vietnam and Korea. In her crouched posture is the promise of peace. The battle marks and ribbons that decorate her record of service show how well she kept that promise.

The *New Jersey* went. She conquered. Now she is back home. And this community welcomes her with great pride and gratitude.

In that spirit, the *Courier-Post* dedicates this book about the *New Jersey* to the people who built her, to those who served aboard her, to those who returned her to the river where she was born. We're proud that our newspaper was part of the process that brought her home.

Dan A. Martin
president and publisher
Courier-Post

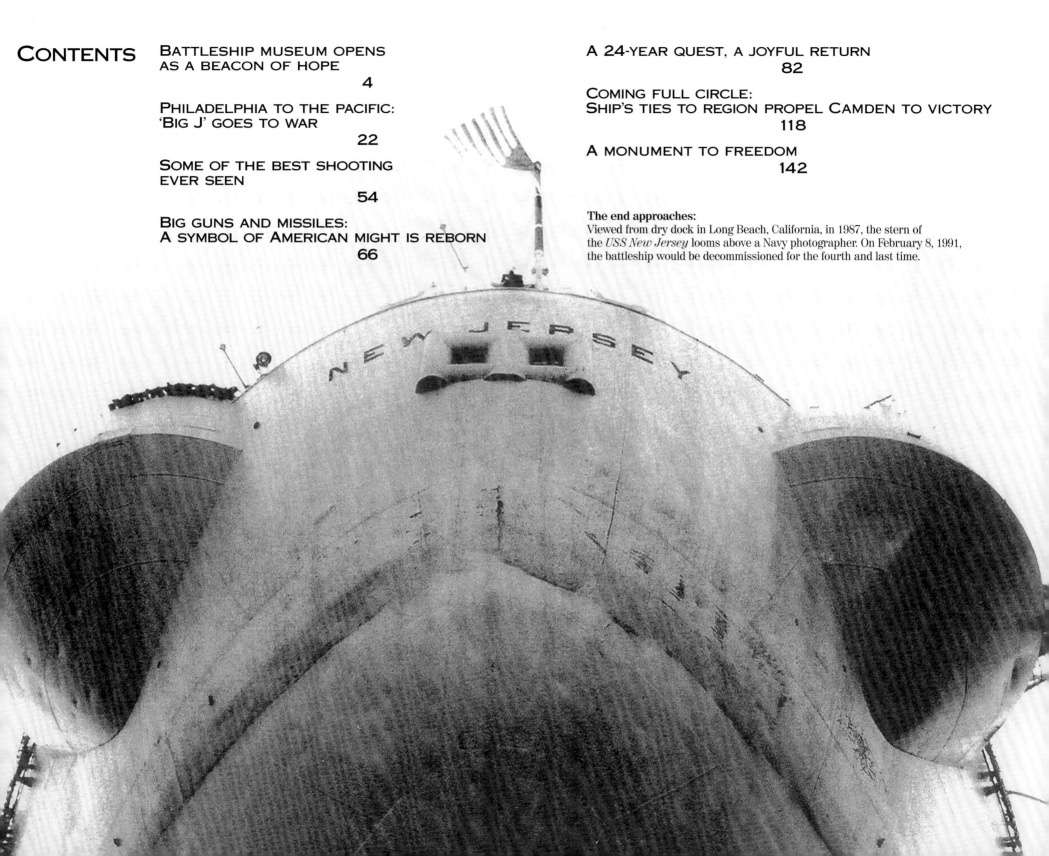

CONTENTS

BATTLESHIP MUSEUM OPENS
AS A BEACON OF HOPE
4

PHILADELPHIA TO THE PACIFIC:
'BIG J' GOES TO WAR
22

SOME OF THE BEST SHOOTING
EVER SEEN
54

BIG GUNS AND MISSILES:
A SYMBOL OF AMERICAN MIGHT IS REBORN
66

A 24-YEAR QUEST, A JOYFUL RETURN
82

COMING FULL CIRCLE:
SHIP'S TIES TO REGION PROPEL CAMDEN TO VICTORY
118

A MONUMENT TO FREEDOM
142

The end approaches:
Viewed from dry dock in Long Beach, California, in 1987, the stern of
the *USS New Jersey* looms above a Navy photographer. On February 8, 1991,
the battleship would be decommissioned for the fourth and last time.

> *"If you doubt America's ability to defend ourselves, just look at this great ship. As it is a warning to our adversaries, let it be a comfort to you."*
>
> – U.S. Sen. Robert Torricelli of New Jersey

BATTLESHIP MUSEUM A BEACON OF HOPE TO A CITY, A NATION

September 2001 – October 2001

With the nation at war for the first time in the 21st century, the aging veteran looked ready for battle – all spit and polished, guns sparkling and positioned for loading.

But this military hero was destined to fight no more.

A new mission at home was calling.

On October 14, 2001, the *USS New Jersey* – the nation's most decorated battleship, a behemoth of unsurpassed size and speed – became the Battleship New Jersey Memorial and Museum.

The *New Jersey* began its final tour of duty quietly secured to a pier on the Delaware River, its big guns and engines long silent but still a powerful and reassuring symbol of American might and resolve.

A crowd of nearly 1,000 invited guests came aboard for the grand opening of the battleship museum at its new and permanent home in Camden, New Jersey, across the river from Philadelphia and the shipyard where the *New Jersey* was built and launched.

The event had the usual features of a patriot-

Acting Gov. Donald DiFrancesco at the museum's grand opening.
CHRIS LACHALL, *Courier-Post*

ic celebration; speeches were delivered, brassy music was performed, cheers went up and tears were shed. But New Jersey State Police troopers with rifles stood guard on the gun turrets and upper decks. Visitors were scanned with hand-held metal detectors. Marine police and firefighters from both Philadelphia and Camden watched from boats. And a flyover by military jets was canceled.

The joy of welcoming visitors aboard to relive the glories of the old warship was tempered by the September 11 terrorist attacks against the nation, which claimed more than 3,000 lives; by a growing anthrax scare of then-undetermined origin; and by fears of still more terrorism.

But the events that shook a nation also strengthened the ship's significance as a monument and museum as it opened its hatches to the public.

"If you doubt America's ability to defend our-

Public officials involved in establishing the Battleship New Jersey Memorial and Museum on the Camden waterfront joyfully celebrate on October 14, 2001. They are (from left) Camden County Surrogate Patricia Jones, U.S. Rep. James H. Saxton, acting New Jersey Gov. Donald DiFrancesco and New Jersey state Sen. John Matheussen.
CHRIS LACHALL, *Courier-Post*

A hijacked airliner heads into the south tower of the World Trade Center in New York on September 11, 2001. Amid fear of new terror attacks, the *USS New Jersey* was moved in secrecy 12 days later to its final berth in Camden, New Jersey.

CARMEN TAYLOR, Associated Press

A fireball erupts as the World Trade Center's south tower is struck by the hijacked airliner. The south tower was the second of the two towers to be hit in the terrorist attacks. Both towers collapsed.

CARMEN TAYLOR, Associated Press

On September 12, 2001, firefighters work around the World Trade Center's destroyed Building No. 7. With the U.S. at war, the battleship *New Jersey's* grand opening celebration as a museum on October 14 contained a somber note.

AVI STEINHARDT, *Courier-Post*

The steel girders of the World Trade Center towers are all that remain of the 110-story buildings on September 12, 2001. The twin towers collapsed less than two hours after the terrorist attack in New York City. The girders were later removed.

AVI STEINHARDT, *Courier-Post*

The *USS New Jersey* was moved in the morning darkness from the Broadway Marine Terminal, where it underwent restoration, to its new home on the Camden waterfront. It was moved on September 23, 2001, without notice to avoid any possibility of a terrorist attack.
BOB RINGHAM, *Courier-Post*

With the Walt Whitman Bridge in the background, tugs tow the *USS New Jersey* up the Delaware River.
CHRIS LACHALL, *Courier-Post*

As the sun rises on September 23, 2001, the majestic battleship makes its way toward its final berth on the Camden waterfront.
CHRIS LACHALL, *Courier-Post*

The *USS New Jersey* is maneuvered into the Delaware River channel as it is eased, stern first, from its Broadway Marine Terminal restoration site in South Camden on September 23, 2001.
RON KARAFIN, *Courier-Post*

selves, just look at this great ship," U.S. Sen. Robert Torricelli of New Jersey told the crowd during a ceremony on the bow, six of the ship's enormous 16-inch guns serving as a backdrop. "As it is a warning to our adversaries, let it be a comfort to you."

In retirement, the *New Jersey* towers majestically more than 150 feet above the waterfront, jutting skyward like a mountaintop. From bow to stern it seems to go on forever, an expanse of steel whose length nearly equals the height of the Eiffel Tower. It sits 200 feet from shore along a 454-foot pier, giving the approaching visitor an enhanced view of its graceful silhouette with its high bow curve sweeping inward from its wide midsection. From its deck, it offers a spectacular view of the Philadelphia skyline.

Even before it opened as a tourist attraction, the *New Jersey* was welcomed as a beacon of hope for Camden, the nation's second poorest city

at the start of the millennium. At the grand opening, acting New Jersey Gov. Donald DiFrancesco spoke of the ship's added role as a beacon of hope for a nation at war.

"The event today comes at a time when our fighting ships are out at sea again, and though she has fired her last shot, maybe this lasting symbol of education and freedom will serve as an inspiration in the country's fight against terrorism from abroad," DiFrancesco said.

The ship began both its first and final missions after surprise attacks on the nation; it was launched in 1942 on the first anniversary of the Japanese bombing of Pearl Harbor. It also had an encounter with modern-day terrorism. One of its sailors, Michael Gorchinski, died in the 1983 Marine barracks bombing in Beirut, Lebanon, which took 241 lives.

The sailor's father was on board for the

With the Philadelphia skyline in the background, the battleship slowly makes its way to its final home on the Camden waterfront.
RON KARAFIN, *Courier-Post*

When she heard the battleship was being moved for the last time during the early morning hours of September 23, 2001, Nancy Robertson of Pennsauken, New Jersey, quickly went to Camden to watch.
BOB RINGHAM, *Courier-Post*

"This is a very emotional day for me. I am proud to be an American and I feel like Mike is still here as part of the ship."

– Ben Gorchinski, father of slain sailor

opening of the *New Jersey* as a museum.

"This is a very emotional day for me," said Ben Gorchinski of Pleasantville, New Jersey, dabbing his eyes with a handker-chief. "I am proud to be an American and I

Michael Gorchinski

feel like Mike is still here as part of the ship."

His son, a chief electronics technician and sur-face warfare spe-cialist, had gone ashore to help Marines with radar equipment. He was in their compound

when it was blown up by terrorists using a truck bomb. Later, some of the ship's crew helped remove bodies and care for the wounded.

The late sailor's wife, Judy Gorchinski, would like to see the *New Jersey* still sailing. "Mike always loved that ship," she said from her home in Sacramento, California. "There are no ships like it. It's an

"I understand the security reasons, but I am not feeling too good right now since we were counting on getting that last ride on it."

– Steve Borkowski,
a Navy veteran who laboriously scraped
paint, lifted equipment and made repairs

Steve Borkowski, a 75-year-old volunteer from Collingswood, New Jersey, shows his disappointment at not being able to be on board the battleship during its trip to its new home. Borkowski had worked on the ship's restoration for nine months. The *USS New Jersey* was moved September 23, 2001, without prior notice to the public, for security reasons.

BOB RINGHAM, *Courier-Post*

The tugboat *James McAllister* leads the *USS New Jersey* to its final berth along the Camden waterfront.
SHAWN SULLIVAN, *Courier-Post*

As the battleship is moved to its new home on the Camden waterfront, Dorsey Rhodes of Camden fishes nearby.
BOB RINGHAM, *Courier-Post*

"It's coming this morning? Get out of here! I've been watching them build this pier since they started. It's one of the greatest ideas they had. I'm going to make it my business to be one of the first ones on that ship."

– Dorsey Rhodes,
upon learning of the ship's move to its final berth

Retired Lt. Cmdr. Robert Elliott served on the battleship from 1942 to 1945. Elliott, a New York resident, visited the *USS New Jersey* in Camden in July 2001, some 56 years after he last saw it.
RON KARAFIN, *Courier-Post*

"They've made some changes since I was aboard, but I quickly found my old state room. I think it's just great what they're doing to make it a museum."

– Retired Lt. Cmdr.
Robert Elliott

Joseph Balzano, executive director of the South Jersey Port Corp. and secretary of the Home Port Alliance board of trustees, was a key figure in the renovation of the *USS New Jersey* and construction of its pier. He checks on pier work, one day after the battleship arrived at its new home.
AVI STEINHARDT, *Courier-Post*

The *USS New Jersey* rests in the Delaware River on the Camden waterfront. It joined other waterfront attractions such as the Tweeter Center, the Children's Garden, the New Jersey State Aquarium, Campbell's Field and a marina.

AVI STEINHARDT, *Courier-Post*

New Jersey Distinguished Service Award medals are set in rows on a table, ready for a private ceremony aboard the *USS New Jersey* on September 25, 2001, honoring 100 veterans from Gloucester County and other New Jersey counties.
AVI STEINHARDT, *Courier-Post*

Guests on the bow of the *USS New Jersey* salute the flag at the grand opening of the Battleship New Jersey Memorial and Museum on October 14, 2001, as two main gun batteries loom before them.
CHRIS LACHALL, *Courier-Post*

intimidating symbol projecting power – awesome."

Her sentiments were shared by many of those who served on the ship. Some drove long distances to attend an opening held with only a few days' notice, partly because of a rush to avoid any more terrorism-related delays.

"It's a sad time with her just sitting here when she shouldn't be. On the other hand, we are happy she has been saved and she looks fabulous," said Steven Cox of Detroit, Michigan, a captain of one of the ship's 5-inch gun mounts during the Beirut crisis. He drove all night to make the opening.

Some of those who built or later overhauled the ship in Philadelphia also were on hand. Sam Mastrogiacomo of Washington Township, New Jersey, helped install its bulkheads. "Sailors say the ship has a soul and I am beginning to believe it myself," said the World War II shipbuilder, a volunteer who helped repair the *New Jersey*.

No high-ranking Navy officials attended the ceremonial opening because of short notice and the war against the ruling Taliban government of Afghanistan.

Robert H. Yancey Sr., of Florence, New Jersey, arrives at the grand opening of the Battleship New Jersey Memorial and Museum on October 14, 2001. "This is something we've been looking forward to for a long time. We finally got it where we want it," said Yancey, a past commander of the New Jersey Disabled American Veterans and a veteran of three wars.
CHRIS LACHALL, *Courier-Post*

> *"It's a sad time with her just sitting here when she shouldn't be. On the other hand, we are happy she has been saved and she looks fabulous."*
>
> – Steven Cox,
> a captain of one of the ship's 5-inch gun mounts during the Beirut crisis

U.S.-led airstrikes began October 7, 2001, after the Taliban refused to surrender Osama bin Laden, the prime suspect in the terror attacks, which leveled the World Trade Center in New York and heavily damaged the Pentagon.

Camden Mayor Gwendolyn Faison welcomed the ship to the city, saying it had "raised the spirit of veterans, the state and the people of Camden." She called the great ship the "best thing that ever happened to Camden."

The same chaplain who offered a prayer at the *New Jersey's* fourth and final decommissioning in 1991 gave the invocation at its rebirth as a museum.

The chaplain, Capt. James P. Nickols of Williamsburg, Virginia, almost shouted the words: "*New Jersey* is here!"

"She is being readied to embark upon a noble mission of connecting Americans to their naval heritage," Nickols said. "Reward *New Jersey's* service to our nation and world with people dedicated to preserving this

Former crew members of the *USS New Jersey,* who served from 1942 through 1991, visit the battleship during the grand opening of the museum on October 14, 2001.

CHRIS LACHALL, *Courier-Post*

mighty battleship. Grant that the *New Jersey* inspire each generation of young men and women to serve our nation in uniform and to consecrate their lives to the values of honor, courage and commitment."

The leaders of the Home Port Alliance, the nonprofit South Jersey group awarded the ship in 2000, praised the hundreds of volunteers who took part in the $22 million restoration project, financed mainly with local, state and federal grants.

"Right now, I would like to reach out and embrace every one of you," Patricia Jones, a Camden County official and Alliance co-chairman, said to the volunteers and other ship supporters. "How often do people see dreams come true?"

Co-chairman John Matheussen, a state senator representing parts of Camden and Gloucester counties, addressed these words to the ship:

"From December 7, 1942, to October 14, 2001 – from birth to berth. May you be a teacher, a reverent memorial and a symbol of America's freedom for yesterday, today and tomorrow."

A moving rendition of "Proud to be an American" by Michael Jones, a singer from Washington Township, New Jersey, brought the crowd to its feet and some audience members to tears. The program ended emotionally with the 63rd Army Band playing and the crowd joining in singing "God Bless America" – the same song sung by Kate Smith when the ship first slid into the Delaware River.

The ship's first visitors were ecstatic it had been saved, preserved in its 1980s configuration. Its restoration received raves.

"Everything is beautiful," said 80-year-old Joe Cesare of Elmira, New York, who served as an electrician's mate on the ship from 1942 to 1944. "It's hard to look at it and not choke up."

State Assemblyman Joseph Azzolina of Monmouth County, chairman of the New Jersey Battleship Commission and its fund-raising foundation, used the occasion to announce that his group would release more money for the ship – $250,000 to help bathe the *New Jersey* in light at night.

"We're here today to bind the people of New Jersey as one – one people, one battleship," Azzolina said. "What a proud and glorious moment, for all of us as we pay tribute to a great warrior."

His call for unity was a reference to the wounds from heated competition in past years between Camden and the North Jersey community of Bayonne for the right to host the ship. The Battleship Commission had backed the Bayonne site.

Robert H. Yancey Sr., of Florence, New Jersey, a past commander of the New Jersey Disabled American Veterans, was impressed with the ship's fresh appearance. "It looks fantastic and we finally got it here where we wanted it," he said.

But original crew member Robert Parmelee of Fort Myers, Florida, a World War II chief radar technician, was not so sure how the ship would fare in Camden. "Most older crew members were in favor of Bayonne, but I think it looks fine here – and still has the sexiest bow in the fleet," he said.

DiFrancesco and others praised the Battleship Commission's nearly 20-year effort to bring the ship to New Jersey, but the governor also said: "Camden is right for the ship and the ship is right for Camden."

Many hoped the ship would give Camden a much-needed economic lift by drawing even more visitors to a waterfront already home to an aquarium, ballpark, entertainment center and marina but still lacking the vibrancy and activity of other reborn East Coast ports.

Retired Navy Capt. David B. McGuigan, the Alliance's first board president and the key person behind its winning application to the Navy, said he hoped the ship would serve as the keystone in the further development of the Camden waterfront.

"You and I collectively must carry out the Alliance's mission statement, the statement we put in our application to the Navy – to create innovative programs that will bring economic progress to the city and have an economic impact on the region," McGuigan told the

Camden County Surrogate Patricia Jones (front, from left), Camden City Mayor Gwendolyn Faison and New Jersey state Sen. John Matheussen cut the ribbon at the public opening of the Battleship New Jersey Memorial and Museum on October 15, 2001.

RON KARAFIN, *Courier-Post*

grand-opening crowd.

The Alliance trustees had targeted a Labor Day opening but that proved too ambitious. They encountered permit delays in the construction of the $1 million landside visitor center, as well as delays in building the $11 million pier.

Secrecy surrounded the September 23 move of the ship from its repair pier in South Camden to its final berth along the downtown waterfront, disappointing the public and those connected with the ship. A planned boat parade could not be held, and there were no crowds to watch the last, 1.5-mile leg of the *New Jersey's* journey to its final berth.

The secrecy was demanded by the Coast Guard, which had delayed the move for 10 days – primarily because it had to focus on port security following the terrorist attacks of September 11. It was the U.S. Coast Guard that chose the day and time – a Sunday morning, just before dawn, when river traffic was minimal and fewer cutters would be needed to create a safety zone.

The Alliance was forced to scrap the ride and onboard party planned for those who served on the ship and hundreds of volunteers who worked on its return to the state and subsequent restoration. Aboard for the short but historic trip were only the Alliance's executive director, Thomas Seigenthaler, 24 line handlers and 12 of the ship's working crew.

The public was not notified of the move until just a few hours before tugboats from McAllister Towing of Camden took the ship on its last voyage, a trip of only 90 minutes. By the time most people were getting up that Sunday, the ship was already at its new location.

Volunteers like Steve Borkowski, a Navy veteran from Collingswood, New Jersey, who had helped scrape paint and make other repairs, were devastated. He raced to the waterfront after he saw an early morning TV newscast about the ship's move.

"I understand the security reasons, but I am not feeling too good right now since we were counting on getting that last ride on it," Borkowski said shortly after arriving at river's edge.

For many, however, the disappointment faded weeks later as the ship welcomed its first visitors.

The *USS New Jersey* would no longer head to sea in harm's way. But the old warrior still had a story to tell.

Philadelphia to the Pacific: The 'Big J' goes to war

September 1940 – June 1948

From the sailors who served aboard the ship to the Marines who watched for it to come over the horizon, the *USS New Jersey* was an awe-inspiring fortress of steel.

Almost the length of three football fields, it was one of a class of four battleships that were the biggest and fastest the United States ever built. If the ship's mere size could stir feelings of hope and pride, its thundering guns could send chills down the spine.

Spewing fireballs as it hurled nearly 2,000-pound shells close to 25 miles, the Big J – as it was called because of its size – also acquired a more colorful nickname: the Black Dragon.

By whatever name, the *New Jersey*, or *Jersey,* was a lucky ship that made much of its own good fortune in war during a career that spanned nearly 50 years.

Starting with World War II, it played a front-line role in virtually every major conflict through 1991, logging hundreds of thousands of sea miles – a record of longevity unmatched in modern naval history.

Remarkably, only one sailor was ever killed in action on the ship – during the Korean War – and the *New Jersey* never received significant damage.

Aided by an armor of steel plate nearly 18 inches thick in places, the *New Jersey* achieved the longest and most enviable service record of any U.S. battleship: 19 campaign stars and other citations.

The *USS New Jersey* was built during the early years of World War II at the now-closed Philadelphia Naval Shipyard, then known as the Philadelphia Navy Yard.

With the Navy seeking to match the ship building of the Japanese, Congress had set aside money for a new fast-ship category of battleship. The giant ships would become known as the *Iowa* class, after the *Iowa,* the first of the class. The *New Jersey*

A 48-star jack flies on the jackstaff in the breeze on the bow of the *New Jersey* at its commissioning on May 23, 1943, at Pier 4 at the Philadelphia Navy Yard, whose name was later changed to Philadelphia Naval Shipyard. The flag is flown only when a Navy ship is in port or anchored. The bow is riding high in the water because ammunition and fuel had not yet been loaded. The *New Jersey* had the longest and most meritorious service record of any U.S. battleship: 19 campaign stars and other citations.

Charles Edison, former Secretary of the Navy and later governor of New Jersey, makes the first weld during the laying of the keel of the *USS New Jersey* on September 16, 1940, at the Philadelphia Naval Shipyard.

Courtesy of the Independence Seaport Museum

Thousands of men watch as workers lay the keel of the *USS New Jersey*.

National Archives photo, courtesy of Home Port Alliance

The 887-foot battleship begins to take shape during the early stages of construction at the now-closed Philadelphia Naval Shipyard. Thousands of welders, painters, riggers, sheet metal workers, carpenters, machinists and engineers worked on the ship. The construction and launch site was later made into a parking lot.

National Archives photo, courtesy of the Home Port Alliance

Workers at the Philadelphia Naval Shipyard continue to work on the *USS New Jersey* on July 8, 1942, in this bow view looking aft. The battleship is just months away from its launching.

The upper rotating assembly of Turret No. 2, consisting of the gun house, gun pit and machinery flat, is lowered into position on the *USS New Jersey* on January 2, 1943.

National Archives photo, courtesy of the Home Port Alliance

Mable McCray (above, right) was one of the women who helped build the battleship. The former welder from Millsboro, Delaware, was among the former shipyard workers who shared her experiences on the *USS New Jersey* during a tour of the ship in early 2001. With her is Marinee Brennan, manager of events and activities for the Home Port Alliance.

AVI STEINHARDT, *Courier-Post*

Officials and spectators are dwarfed by the *USS New Jersey* in this view of the bow during its launching at the Philadelphia Naval Shipyard on December 7, 1942, the first anniversary of the Japanese attack on Pearl Harbor, Hawaii.

National Archives photo, courtesy of the Home Port Alliance

LAUNCHING OF BB-62. VIEW OF BOW. NAVY YARD, PHILA. DEC. 7-1942.

Workers and officials take a look at the hull's stern prior to the ship's launching at the Philadelphia Naval Shipyard on December 7, 1942. Three of the four propeller shafts are visible, each as thick as a man's torso.

National Archives photo, courtesy of the Home Port Alliance

Mable Giordano of Mount Ephraim, New Jersey, worked on the *USS New Jersey* as a welder in the Philadelphia shipyard's pipe shop. She was among the many former workers who came to see the Big J come home to the Delaware River, after its journey from Bremerton, Washington.

RON KARAFIN, *Courier-Post*

"Oh, the splash she made in the water! She slid down into the river real nice as if she was glad to get a bath in the river."

– Mable Giordano,
a shipbuilder who worked as
a welder in the Philadelphia shipyard's pipe shop

Two original members of the ship's crew, John Horan of Cherry Hill, New Jersey (above, left), and Russell Collins of Palmyra, New Jersey, visit the site on the Camden waterfront chosen for the battleship, months before it was moved there to serve as a floating museum.

AL SCHELL, *Courier-Post*

Carolyn Edison, wife of then-New Jersey Gov. Charles Edison, christened the *USS New Jersey* on December 7, 1942. It was her husband, the son of inventor Thomas Edison of Menlo Park, New Jersey, who had the ship named for the state when he served as acting Secretary of the Navy for President Franklin Roosevelt in 1939.

Carolyn Edison breaks the champagne bottle on the bow of the *USS New Jersey* at the christening of the battleship on December 7, 1942 at the Philadelphia Naval Shipyard. As the ship slid into the Delaware River, Mrs. Edison blew the ship kisses with both hands.

A massive propeller of the *USS New Jersey* is shown in dry dock in September 1967. The battleship has four propellers, two inboard that are five-bladed and 17 feet in diameter. The other two are outboard, four-bladed and reach 18 feet, 3 inches in diameter.

Thousands of men and women, both on board and off, watch as the mammoth battleship makes its splash into the Delaware River during its launching from the Philadelphia Naval Shipyard on December 7, 1942. During the 60-second trip, its whistle tooted and black smoke emerged from one of its two stacks in a show staged by the yard using a portable steam generator and oily rags. Launching is a delicate operation. The weight of the vessel has to be transferred from the keel blocks, shoring timbers and other fixed supports to the sliding ways, which carry the ship down the ground ways into the water. The ways are heavily greased skids that facilitate the ship's movement when the release mechanism, or trigger, releases the vessel.

National Archives photo, courtesy of the Home Port Alliance

Sailors salute the flag during commissioning ceremonies in Philadelphia on May 23, 1943. From May to December, the battleship underwent a fitting out and initial training in the Western Atlantic and Caribbean.
Courtesy of Robert Elliott

Sailors on the fantail of the *USS New Jersey* create a sea of white during commissioning ceremonies in Philadelphia on May 23, 1943. It had a crew of nearly 3,000 under the command of Capt. Carl F. Holden and carried a detachment of Marines.
Courtesy of Robert Elliott

"Today this inanimate 'it' becomes a 'she', a being endowed with the living character of personality, with a soul and with a purpose. A lovely lady, but a lovely lady who will have her angry moments."

– Capt. Carl F. Holden,
at commissioning, May 23, 1943

Officials and guests celebrate the commissioning of the ship with refreshments served on the *New Jersey's* silver service.
Courtesy of Robert Elliott

The *USS New Jersey* sits at anchor off a western Pacific Ocean atoll in July 1945. Other ships of the fleet wait nearby for the signal to move out in another lightning thrust against enemy-held islands. For a year and a half before this picture was taken, the battleship had been having its own way in the Pacific, the U.S. Navy said. In one operation after another, beginning with the Marshall Islands and running straight through to the first airstrikes on Tokyo, the Big J had gone about the business of leveling Japanese shore installations and protecting carrier forces.

Courtesy of the United States Naval Institute

"Hit hard, hit fast, hit often and get out fast. We get away with it because we violate all traditional rules of naval warfare. We do the exact opposite of what they expect us to do."

– Adm. William "Bull" Halsey

Adm. William "Bull" Halsey sits in his chair on the Flag Bridge of the *USS New Jersey* as it steams toward the Philippines in December 1944. The battleship served in the Third Fleet as the flagship of Halsey, a native of Elizabeth, New Jersey.

Courtesy of the United States Naval Institute

Capt. Carl F. Holden (left) and other officers of the *USS New Jersey* discuss preparations for the commissioning ceremony for the battleship on May 23, 1943.

Capt. Carl F. Holden stands on the deck of the battleship. Holden was the ship's first commanding officer.

Lt. Cmdr. Robert Elliott (seated, far right) and members of the Damage Control Department of the *USS New Jersey* pose for a staff picture on the battleship's deck. Elliott served as the ship's damage control officer during World War II. Others in the department included (seated, from left) Lt. Davidson, Lt. Cmdr. Howe, department head Cmdr. Addison and Lt. Cmdr. Hodge. Standing, from left, are Chief Boatswain Scitowski, Ensign Lutmen, Lt. (jg) McCaffery, Ensign Deal, Chief Warrant Hull and Warrant Gavrell. The first names of the staff members were unavailable.

Sailors on board the *USS New Jersey* take a break from the rigors of fighting in World War II. Two unidentified men take in the sun on top of the twin 5-inch gun mounts.
Courtesy of Robert Elliott

Crew members of the battleship relax on the main deck forward of Turret No. 1 in July 1943. The *USS New Jersey* was on sea trials in the Atlantic Ocean off New Jersey before heading to the Pacific Theatre in World War II.
Courtesy of Robert Elliott

Life on the *USS New Jersey* had its lighter moments. In the 1950s, the men on the battleship relax in their bunks, some reading, others writing home or just chatting. The compact living conditions were the norm for all ships up through the post-Korean War period.
National Archives photo, courtesy of the Home Port Alliance

Messmen serve food in the galley of the *USS New Jersey* on November 3, 1950.

National Archives photo, courtesy of the Home Port Alliance

Ship's servicemen strikers John Nelencamp (left) and Charles Manley wash clothing in the laundry of the *USS New Jersey* in January 1952.

National Archives photo, courtesy of the Home Port Alliance

The Big J was *"just about the biggest thing in the world."* The tour on the ship would become *"days of pure monotony highlighted by days of pure anxiety."*

– Edgar Hill, one of the few crew members who was on board the ship when it was launched

was to come next, followed by the *Wisconsin* and the *Missouri*. Two other *Iowa* ships were started – the *Kentucky* at Norfolk, Virginia, and the *Illinois* at Philadelphia – but were never completed and were scrapped after World War II.

The 1921 Washington Naval Treaty limited naval shipbuilding by the United States, Great Britain, France, Italy and Japan. But U.S. intelligence reports indicated the Japanese were building new and larger battleships in the late 1930s in apparent violation of the treaty. To maintain parity, the United States decided to build the *Iowa*-class ships, gaining permission from the treaty board after most nations – but not Japan – signed a new pact, the 1936 London Naval Treaty.

The American ships turned out to be faster than the Japanese ships, including the *Yamato,* though the United States did not know it at the time. But the guns on the Japanese warships were bigger – 18 inches – which also came as a surprise. U.S. naval planners had opted to stay at 16 inches rather than giving up speed or greatly raising the costs of the ships.

Numbered BB-62, the *New Jersey* was authorized by Congress in 1938 along with the *Iowa*. Contracts were awarded a year later. With war raging in Europe, but the United States still on the sidelines, the ship's keel was laid on September 16, 1940.

The Philadelphia shipyard was teeming with workers during the war years – hitting peak employment of nearly 60,000. From Pennsylvania, southern New Jersey and Delaware came welders, painters, riggers, sheet metal workers, carpenters, machinists and engineers. All took great care and pride in their work.

Because the shipyard had never built a ship as large as the *New Jersey*, a few problems occurred. At its launch, the ship hit the Jersey shore and had to be rescued by tugboats.

The general preparation for the inevitable U.S. entry into World War II required retooling yard equipment and facilities; the construction of two of the yard's largest dry docks, No. 4 and No. 5; and the addition of two ship-building ways, or skids. The *New Jersey* was built on an older pair of shipbuilding ways lengthened by more than 300 feet to accommodate the larger ship. The ways were built on an incline to enable a gravity launching.

In addition, the shipyard had to train more welders and other craftsmen, install large cranes to lift the massive gun turrets, and build a new foundry to make some of the larger castings required for the ship.

"This made it into a major shipyard, with first-class production, in which about one-third of the work force came from across the river in southern New Jersey," said Professor Jeffrey Dorwart of Rutgers University in Camden, New Jersey. He is the author of *The Philadelphia Navy Yard: From the Birth of the U.S. Navy to the Nuclear Age.*

"Even in World War II when there were ships all over the place, the *New Jersey* struck people when they saw it – and not just Navy people," Dorwart said. "They thought it was something special. It created an excitement and stirred more interest and pride than any other ship."

The *Iowa*-class ships were the "Navy's version of the atomic bomb," Dorwart said.

"It was at the time the ultimate weapon – the perfect surface warship. It is perfectly balanced in every way and its hull is designed for maximum speed," he said.

After the launching, topside work was completed while the ship was in dry dock. The ship then was moved to Pier 4, where the 16-inch turrets were lifted on board and the bridge superstructure was built. It was there that a spectacular fire erupted during rewelding of the conning towers. The welds had cracked during the winter. The blaze did little damage.

By 1942, the ship's first crewmen started arriving and helped finish the ship.

John Borek was a sheet metal worker at the ship-

Crew member Sal Cusumano purchases items from Edward Coletti, storekeeper 3rd class, in the ship's store in 1952.

National Archives photo, courtesy of the Home Port Alliance

"There was the camaraderie and pride to be on the biggest and best, and being mostly teenagers, it was for us an exciting adventure."

– John Horan, original crewman

Hearing from loved ones was sure to bring smiles to crew members of the *USS New Jersey*. Here, a working party handles incoming mailbags.
National Archives photo, courtesy of the Home Port Alliance

yard. One of his jobs was fashioning the steel on the elevators that carried gunpowder from the storage magazine at the bottoms of the gun turrets to the guns above.

"We used to pull the nylons over metal parts to see if they would catch on anything and get runs in them," said Borek, of Winslow, New Jersey. "This way we knew there were still rough spots on the metal we had to remove.

"She's a beautiful ship. They will never again make anything like her. She was the answer to a GI's prayer when she would come over the horizon into view."

Women helped build the ship, too. "You got a feeling you never had before because you did something as a woman that no other woman had done," said Mable McCray of Millsboro, Delaware, who worked as a welder.

The Japanese attack on Pearl Harbor on December 7, 1941, sped up construction of the $100 million ship. Eight-hour days were replaced by 12-hour shifts, enabling the Navy to launch the ship on a date with special significance: Pearl Harbor's one-year anniversary.

Entertainer Kate Smith belted out "God Bless America" to an estimated 20,000 onlookers. Carolyn Edison, wife of then-New Jersey Gov. Charles Edison, christened the ship by breaking a champagne bottle on its bow. It was Governor Edison, the son of inventor Thomas Edison of Menlo Park, New Jersey, who had the ship named for the state when he served as acting Secretary of the Navy for President Franklin Roosevelt in 1939.

As the *New Jersey* slid into the Delaware River on greased ways, Mrs. Edison blew the ship kisses with both hands. During the 60-second trip, the ways smoked from

A crewman checks the control panel in the main battery plot of the *USS New Jersey*. The controls could set up different combinations of directors, guns and range keepers.

Fireman John M. Hernandez (from left), Machinist Mate Fireman James Cronin and Machinist Mate Fireman Robert E. Plank stand watch in an engine room. The men are operating the throttle and relaying orders by sound-powered telephones to the other engine rooms.

National Archives photo, courtesy of the Home Port Alliance

the friction, the ship's whistle tooted and black smoke emerged from one of the two stacks in a show staged by the yard using a portable steam generator and oily rags. Its momentum unexpectedly carried the 887-foot ship across the Delaware River to the New Jersey shoreline, creating a wave that swamped spectators at the water's edge, said Edgar Hill of Westville, New Jersey, who was aboard the ship at the time.

To Hill, the Big J was "just about the biggest thing in the world." His tour on the ship would become "days of pure monotony highlighted by days of pure anxiety."

"Oh, the splash she made in the water! She slid down into the river real nice as if she was glad to get a bath in the river," said Mable Giordano of Mount Ephraim, New Jersey, another of the ship's builders. She worked as a welder in the Philadelphia shipyard's pipe shop.

The *New Jersey*, which was capable of top speeds of over 33 knots (about 38 mph), was commissioned in Philadelphia on May 23, 1943. It had a crew of nearly 3,000, carried a detachment of Marines and was under the command of Capt. Carl F. Holden, whose concern for his crew gained him the high regard of his men.

Russell Collins of Palmyra, New Jersey, an original crew member, remembers its first trip through the Panama Canal.

"We had never seen anything up close that was that big before and I remember when we went through the canal you could reach out and touch the palm trees – that's how little clearance there was on the sides of the canal locks," he said.

Crew members man the Mark 4, 20mm guns of the *USS New Jersey* while at sea in 1943. Although considered short-range automatic weapons, the aircraft guns could fire to a maximum range of 4,800 yards and an altitude of 10,000 feet.

Courtesy of Robert Elliott

Sailors clean and grease 40mm gun rounds on board the *USS New Jersey* in December 1944. As an attacking aircraft closed in on the battleship, anti-aircraft fire increased in volume. The 5-inch guns with proximity-fuse rounds were fired, followed by 40mm recoil-operated heavy machine guns and 20mm aircraft guns.

Crew members man the 40mm guns of the *USS New Jersey* while at sea in 1943. The guns could fire to a maximum range of 11,000 yards and an altitude of 22,800 feet.

"Sweeper man your brooms, clean sweep down, fore and aft," was heard twice a day on the battleship. With brooms in hand, crewmen clean the deck of the *USS New Jersey*.

Radarman Seaman E.E. Lockley operates a radar repeater in the Combat Information Center on board the battleship in September 1953. The 1980s modernization of the ship upgraded the CIC, which is now referred to as the Combat Engagement Center.
National Archives photo, courtesy of the Home Port Alliance

A destroyer (foreground) and two aircraft carriers are part of the *USS New Jersey*'s task force, as seen from the camera of a sailor on board the Big J during World War II.
Courtesy of Robert Elliott

Occasionally, the huge fuel reserves of the battleship served other ships while at sea. Hundreds of men on board the *USS New Jersey* (right) watch as it refuels the Allen M. Sumner-class destroyer *USS Borie* on March 16, 1945. A K-gun with depth-charge loaded and a ready service rack of depth charges are visible on the *Borie's* main deck.

The deck crew handles the lines as the *USS New Jersey* refuels the destroyer *USS Lewis Hancock* in December 1944.
National Archives photo, courtesy of the Home Port Alliance

Crew members sit on the forward 16-inch main battery fire control director. The director is equipped with an early World War II fire control radar. Its antenna is clearly visible atop the director.
Courtesy of Robert Elliott

Halsey's motto: "Hit hard, hit fast, hit often and get out fast."

"We get away with it because we violate all traditional rules of naval warfare," he said. "We do the exact opposite of what they expect us to do."

Being on a battleship was "the ultimate for a sailor," remembered John Horan of Cherry Hill, New Jersey, a member of the original crew.

"There was camaraderie and pride to be on the biggest and best, and being mostly teenagers, it was for us an exciting adventure," the former signalman said.

When its 16-inch guns fired, no hands could be on the main deck though some were at their stations on upper decks. "The ship vibrated, and the heat and percussion from the booms were awesome. Sometimes deck fittings were blown off," said former crewman Collins.

The *New Jersey* began its World War II campaign supporting carrier air strikes against the Kwajalein and Eniwetok atolls in the Marshall Islands on January 29, 1944. In the attack on a Japanese naval base at Truk in the Caroline Islands, it sank one ship and damaged several others. It also screened carriers with anti-aircraft fire during the Battle of Philippine Sea, often called the Marianas Turkey Shoot, in which the Japanese lost 400 planes.

The ship also participated as part of Task Force 38 in the largest naval battle of the war at Leyte Gulf in the Philippines, starting on October 23, 1944. But it never got to fire a shot from its big guns. Because Halsey was duped into going for a decoy Japanese fleet to the north, the *New Jersey* never dueled with the largest Japanese battleships that were part of the large Japanese naval forces at Leyte.

The Japanese suffered a major blow and could never again mount a formidable naval action against the Americans, who achieved naval superiority as a result of Leyte.

On October 29, the *New Jersey* shot down one of several kamikazes, Japanese suicide planes, that attacked her formation en masse. It crashed onto the port gun galleries of the carrier *USS Intrepid*. During this action, three of the *New Jersey*'s crewmen were wounded by friendly machine gun fire from the *Intrepid*.

In December, the Big J was with the carrier *Lexington* in a task force striking against Luzon in the Philippines – until the task force found itself in the

Reaching the war in the Pacific in 1944 after passing through the Panama Canal, the *New Jersey* helped protect aircraft carriers in battle groups and bombarded islands held by the Japanese. It served first in the Fifth Fleet as the flagship of Adm. Raymond Spruance, who was a hero of the decisive Battle of Midway, which occurred in 1942 before the *Iowa*-class battleships entered the war. The *New Jersey* also served in the Third Fleet as the flagship of Adm. William "Bull" Halsey, a more unorthodox leader and a native of Elizabeth, New Jersey.

The Big J's nine 16-inch and 20 5-inch guns, combined with its 40mm and 20mm anti-aircraft weapons, shot down planes, sank ships and pummeled enemy-occupied islands. Hurling projectiles weighing the equivalent of a Volkswagen Beetle, the ship's big guns inflicted heavy damage and killed thousands of Japanese.

In a gun practice, New Jersey crewmen exercise 20mm and 5-inch guns. Rigorous practice in loading, training, elevating and sighting enabled the gun crews to achieve the weapons' optimum capabilities, 800 rounds per minute on the 20mm and 15 to 20 rounds per minute on the 5-inch guns.

The *USS New Jersey*'s three observation/scout planes, Vought OS2U Kingfishers, ride on the fantail on September 3, 1943, during its voyage from Trinidad to Hampton Roads, Virginia. The planes' cockpits are covered to protect them from the sea. The aircraft were catapulted from the fantail of the battleship. On their return, they landed on the water and were retrieved by the aircraft crane on the stern.

National Archives photo, courtesy of the Home Port Alliance

midst of a typhoon. Three destroyers capsized, but the *New Jersey* rode out the storm without damage.

During most of 1945, the ship island-hopped in the Pacific, bombarding Okinawa, Formosa, Luzon and Wake Island and providing protection for carriers and other ships.

The ship's damage control officer, Lt. Cmdr. Robert Elliott of New York City, was like many crewmen. He had requested duty on the *New Jersey*.

"She was a big and beautiful yacht. I was greatly attracted to her and she turned out to be a very safe ship," he said, calling his service during World War II a "special time in my life."

When firing its guns, "the ship quivered from stem to stern," he said.

Elliott also served as the nightly newscaster for the ship's on-board radio station, providing world news every night. He focused, of course, on the war, informing the crew of such major developments as the death of President Franklin Roosevelt.

He recalled that the ship weathered three typhoons "that were worse than any battle."

On one dark and rainy night at sea when ships had to operate without running lights, the *New Jersey* collided with another ship in its task force – the *USS Franks*, a destroyer that had tried to cross the bow of the much larger battleship.

While the Big J was unscathed, its bow sliced into the

Crew members stand on the deck of the *USS New Jersey* as an OS2U Kingfisher floatplane gets ready to be catapulted in 1944.
Courtesy of Robert Elliott

On July 20, 1943, an OS2U Kingfisher floatplane is catapulted to starboard on the *USS New Jersey* while it was in the Delaware Bay for familiarization trials.
National Archives photo, courtesy of the Home Port Alliance

The OS2U Kingfisher floatplane leaves the catapult from the *USS New Jersey* in 1944.
National Archives photo, courtesy of the Home Port Alliance

The OS2U Kingfisher is hoisted from the sea by the aircraft crane on the battleship's stern. The faster, more powerful SC-1 Seahawks, replaced the Kingfishers by 1945.

National Archives photo, courtesy of the Home Port Alliance

Franks like a knife, toppling its bridge and killing the *Franks'* captain. If the *New Jersey* had not turned at the last moment to try to avoid the crash, it might have sliced the *Franks* in half, according to some of its officers and other crew.

A sailor aboard the *Franks*, Michael Back of Surf City, New Jersey, recalled the April 2, 1945, accident.

"We had been out rescuing downed pilots and had to get back into position with our other ships. Somebody made a big (navigational) mistake. The accident happened when we were cutting across the formation and ran into the battleship. The anchor of the *New Jersey* ripped our bridge apart, and its bow made a lengthwise cut along the length of our ship," he said.

Back said he was below deck in his undershorts and thought the ship had hit a torpedo or mine. "There were a lot of sparks around and an explosion. It was terrifying, so in about 10 seconds I made it topside, where everyone was running around screaming," he said.

During the war, the Marines aboard the *New Jersey* manned some of the 20mm anti-aircraft guns and a 5-inch gun mount.

"It was fantastic duty and the Marines played an important role on the ship," said James Schatzman of Del Haven, New Jersey, a former Marine who was from Southwest Philadelphia. He was an orderly for the executive officer when he was not at his battle station.

"It was the whole atmosphere of pride that you were going to be a part of the Navy and playing a role," Schatzman said. "I had never been to sea and couldn't steer a rowboat."

The ship's Damage Control Officer, Lt. Cmdr. Robert Elliott of New York City, was like many crewmen. He had requested duty on the *USS New Jersey* and served during World War II from 1942 to 1945. He also served as the newscaster for the ship's on-board radio station, providing world news every night.

Courtesy of Robert Elliott

Elliott (above, right), and his friends, Lt. Cmdr. Howe (left) and Lt. (jg) McCaffery, manage to take a short break on the shores of Kwajalein atoll in the Pacific.

Courtesy of Robert Elliott

Elliott sees his altered stateroom on the *USS New Jersey* in July 2001 for the first time in 56 years. Elliott was among several former crewmen who took a tour of the ship while it was under restoration at the Broadway Marine Terminal in Camden, before it was moved to its final berth on the Camden waterfront.

RON KARAFIN, *Courier-Post*

"The ship quivered from stem to stern. The guns also broke hundreds of light bulbs. When we later went ashore, we saw that the palm trees were almost all eradicated and the Japanese fortresses gone."

– Retired Lt. Cmdr. Robert Elliott

Japanese prisoners were picked up by the destroyer *Marshall* on September 12, 1944. They were then transported to the *USS New Jersey*, where their heads were shaved and deloused, and they were given new clothing.

Courtesy of Robert Elliott

The *USS New Jersey* makes a high-speed run while en route from Guantanamo Bay, Cuba, to Norfolk, Virginia, on March 16, 1951. The catapults have been removed from the fantail and a canvas-shrouded helicopter sits amid the ship's boats.

Courtesy of the United States Naval Institute

The *USS New Jersey* began its World War II campaign supporting carrier air strikes against the Kwajalein and Eniwetok atolls on January 29, 1944. The devastation on Kwajalein atoll could almost pass for a scene of Nagasaki after it was hit by the atomic bomb.
Courtesy of Robert Elliott

A rifle-like barrel for a 16-inch gun on Turret No. 1 of the *USS New Jersey* has a 2.5-inch outer casing made of specially treated steel. The barrel is composed of several concentric cylindrical pieces shrunk one over the other, and is commonly referred to as a built-up gun. The outer cylinders, or hoops, are heated and assembled one at a time on the tube. As the hoops cool, they shrink and tightly grip the inner cylinders. This assemblage and heat treatment give the barrel the required strength to withstand the internal high pressure built up when the gun is fired.
National Archives photo, courtesy of the Home Port Alliance

One of his comrades in the detachment, Joe Dinell of Fort Worth, Texas, manned a 20mm gun on the bow. He remembers the first time a Japanese Zero came swooping in over the ship.

"A Sergeant Hartley was the air defense officer. He started running but forgot his headset cord only went so far and ended up landing on his back, but he was OK. We joked about it later," Dinell said.

Steaming between Pacific islands, in preparation for what was to have been an invasion of the Japanese mainland, the *New Jersey* was not in Tokyo Bay at the time of the surrender in 1945.

To the disappointment of those serving on the *New Jersey*, President Harry S. Truman chose the *Missouri* as the ship on which the Japanese would surrender, even though the Big J had the most distinguished service record of any *Iowa*-class battleship. The *Missouri* had been christened by Truman's daughter as well as named for his home state.

The Big J did go on, however, to serve as the flag ship and communication headquarters for the occupation forces, under the command of Admiral Spruance.

The battleship left Tokyo Bay in 1946. After an overhaul at Puget Sound Naval Shipyard in Bremerton, Washington, the *New Jersey* was mothballed in Bayonne, New Jersey, across the harbor from New York City, and decommissioned on June 30, 1948.

For valiant performance in the war, during which it logged 200,000 miles, the *New Jersey* was awarded nine battle stars, later officially known as campaign stars. Entering the war earlier than the Big J, the smaller battleship *North Carolina* and the light cruiser *San Diego* each earned 15 stars, and the aircraft carrier *Enterprise* 20 stars.

But the Big J still had a long career ahead.

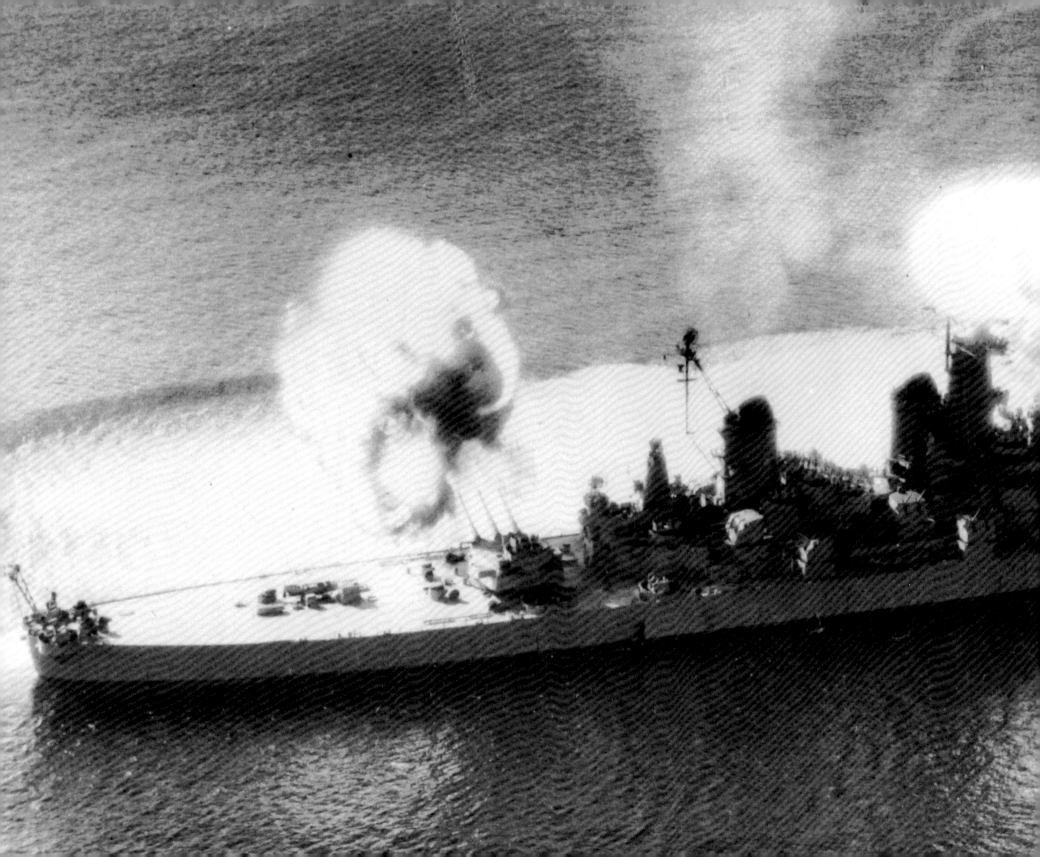

"I have heard firecrackers and gunshots, but the sound of a 16-inch gun going off can't compare. You can't imagine the noise and concussion. You can feel and hear the thunderous sound – not just a quick boom, but a very long one."

– Vincent Falso, gunnery crew, Korean War

SOME OF THE BEST SHOOTING EVER SEEN

November 1950 – December 1969

Just two years after being deactivated, the *New Jersey* was again called to duty. The Big J and its big guns were needed off the coast of Korea.

Recommissioned at Bayonne, New Jersey, on November 21, 1950, the *New Jersey* became the flagship of the Seventh Fleet. It also carried the personal flag of its former flag officer, William "Bull" Halsey, who had been made fleet admiral.

The Korean War was five months old.

The ship steamed off to the Pacific for the first of two tours of duty in the war between communist forces in the North and the Republic of Korea. The *New Jersey* would go on to earn four more battle stars for its service.

The battleship began bombarding Korea in a nighttime attack on Wonsan Harbor on May 20, 1951. It was during that siege the ship suffered its first and only combat death. During a duel that continued into the following day, a North Korean shore gun battery hit Turret No. 1, and a near miss on the port side exploded on the stern, killing Seaman Robert Osterwind of Detroit and seriously wounding two others.

The *USS New Jersey* unleashes a nine 16-inch gun salvo at North Korea in November 1951. The spectacular scene, captured by Chief Aviation Photographer's Mate Patrick Cady, shows the blast's effect on the water.
Courtesy of the United States Naval Institute

55

Vincent Falso said he and other crew members first noticed splashes in the water alongside the ship but heard nothing. Then came the explosions and the realization the ship was being bombarded by a gun battery ashore.

"I was already at my station on a 40mm gun mount when Osterwind was coming up from below decks to report to his gunnery station on the same level as myself. The shrapnel caught him as he was climbing a ladder from the main deck up to his station," said Falso, a gunner turned ship's baker who was born in Westfield, New Jersey, raised in Rhode Island, then moved back to Mountainside, New Jersey.

"The crew was despondent over it, but we had to go on. We went to other harbors but returned to shell Wonsan Harbor many times."

In attacks north of the 38th parallel from Wonsan to Kansong and Chongjin, the ship destroyed bridges, railroads, highways, ammunition dumps and gun positions with pinpoint accuracy, killing thousands of enemy troops. The official Navy history carries the reports of gunspotters who described the ship's firing as "on the nose" and "some of the best shooting ever seen."

Having sailed 49,000 miles on this first deployment, which lasted six months, the *New Jersey* left for home in November 1951. It arrived a month later in Norfolk, Virginia, for an overhaul.

The ship returned to serve again off Korea from April 1953 until the signing of the armistice on July 27, 1953, inflicting major damage to Wonsan at the close of a more than two-year naval siege of the port. With the truce signed, the ship left for home again.

Korean War veterans remembered the beloved ship in the same way as their predecessors.

"There was a special camaraderie and pride being a battleship sailor that you did not feel on other ships," said Robert Walters of Cinnaminson, New Jersey, who served in the ship's navigation department after the Korean War.

A 1953 visit by the Big J to Hong Kong, at the end of its duty in Korea, drew huge crowds and made heroes of two enlisted men. A Chinese work boat capsized as its operator, a woman with an infant daughter, was ferrying sightseers to the ship. Seaman Ronald Delledonne of

A crewman cleans a 16-inch gun barrel on the *USS New Jersey* in 1951.

Courtesy of the United States Naval Institute

The front page of the September 15, 1950, edition of the *Courier-Post* tells its readers of the U.S. Marine assault forces storming the beaches of Inchon, Korea, under the command of General Douglas MacArthur.
Courier-Post archives

"There's nothing like being a battleship sailor. It's like I died and went to heaven."

– Robert Walters,
Korean War era crewman

Ordnance for the 16-inch guns of the *USS New Jersey* are loaded as the crew swings the huge projectiles aboard at Sasebo, Japan, in July 1951.
National Archives photo, courtesy of the Home Port Alliance

Homestead, Pennsylvania, and Pfc. Steven G. Peliotes, a Marine from Muskegon, Michigan, rescued the six who fell overboard, including the infant, who was plucked from beneath the overturned boat by Delledonne.

After a Mediterranean cruise, the Big J was deactivated at the New York Naval Shipyard in Brooklyn and returned to Bayonne for decommissioning once again on August 21, 1957.

Ten years would pass before it sailed again.

A civil war in Vietnam had erupted and the battleship *New Jersey* was needed. It was chosen over the three other *Iowa*-class ships because it had been regunned and was considered in the best condition.

But before it could return to the Pacific, it had to be modernized.

The *New Jersey*, which had been sitting in mothballs at the Philadelphia Naval Shipyard, received new radar and electronics to detect missiles and jam their signals, improved communications, weaponry and, for the first time, air conditioning. A helicopter landing pad also was added to accommodate several types of helicopters, including the H-1 "Hueys," which replaced seaplanes.

With this modernization, far fewer crew members would be required – 1,626 instead of the nearly 3,000 during World War II, providing

Vincent Falso was a gunner turned ship's baker who served on the *USS New Jersey* during the Korean War (above). In 1951, cooks and bakers from the battleship went on rest and recreation in Hawaii (left), where they spent time on the beaches. The R&R was typical of a sailor's liberty.
Courtesy of Vincent Falso

The parents of Seaman Robert Osterwind of Detroit (above, left and center) receive a drawing of their son from a Navy man. Osterwind was the first and only combat death on the *USS New Jersey*. He died in May 1951, during an attack at Wonsan Harbor. A North Korean shore gun battery hit Turret No. 1, and a near miss on the port side exploded on the stern. Osterwind was killed by shrapnel from the blast on the stern.
Courtesy of Vincent Falso

the crew a lot more elbow room.

"I remember like it was yesterday seeing her. I moved equipment out of the engine rooms and marveled at the thickness of the steel in its hull and superstructure," said Jack Cleaver of Brooklawn, New Jersey, who was a shipyard rigger.

Some of those working on the ship had been apprentice craftsmen during World War II.

The *New Jersey* went on to play a limited role during the Vietnam War, at a time when it was the only battleship serving at sea. Arriving on September 29, 1968, at Danang, the ship began firing its guns the next day, damaging targets near the Demilitarized Zone as it sought to protect U.S. servicemen and intimidate the enemy.

"We were there to support the Army and Marine ground troops with firepower and that's what we did very successfully," said Edward Snyder of McLean, Virginia, who was the commanding officer. "Many of them wrote home saying that if it weren't for the *New Jersey*, the enemy would have zapped their asses."

Ronald Dash of Willingboro, New Jersey, was one of those Marines. "When we were heavily attacked," he said, "the *New Jersey* came in with her fire support and saved us and we will never forget it."

Many of the Marines, however, never saw the ship – just the damage it inflicted. But Marvin Cropper of Williamstown, New Jersey, a sailor aboard a Navy destroyer, remembers watching the *New Jersey* firing its guns.

"Our ship and another had been shelling Tiger Island near the DMZ for five-and-a-half months because North Vietnamese had set up missiles there," Cropper said. "The *New Jersey* came over and with two shots from 22 miles out, wiped the island right off the map."

Ken Kersch of Monmouth Junction, New Jersey, was aboard the *New Jersey* during the Vietnam War. He worked in the machine shop, making repair parts.

"The war – it was a job to do. It was a crappy time. We didn't ask to be there," Kersch said.

Kersch was already a crew member when the ship was commissioned in 1968 in Philadelphia, where war protesters staged demonstrations aboard boats on the Delaware River.

"It was a war run by the politicians, not by the military, and when we went home, there were no parades," Kersch said. "You were almost afraid to wear your uniform, except on a military facility."

But during his tour, Kersch said, the sailors were treated well. He said Captain Snyder converted two old gun tubs into small swimming pools for the sailors.

Helicopters were coming and going from the ship so often that Snyder had a sign posted on the helicopter deck reading: "*New Jersey* International."

The commanding officer sometimes brought groups of fighting Marines on board for rest, medical attention and three square meals a day.

Like many of its skippers, Snyder regarded his tour on the Big J as the highlight of his career.

The *USS New Jersey* is moved to a new berth at Pier 4 at the Philadelphia Naval Shipyard on June 11, 1967. Before heading to the Pacific in 1968, the New Jersey received improved electronics, weapons and, for the first time, air conditioning. A helicopter landing pad also was added on the stern.

Courtesy of the United States Naval Institute

Broken only by brief visits to the Philippines for replenishment, the battleship ranged up and down the coast, delivering its massive punch wherever needed.

Firing its guns for the last time on March 31, 1969, the ship was ordered home for refurbishment; following a two-day visit to Japan, the *New Jersey* was back at sea. After a brief diversion, it arrived at Long Beach Naval Shipyard in California on May 5.

As the crew prepared the ship for another deployment in the summer of 1969, the Pentagon released a list of ships to be deactivated for economic reasons. The *New Jersey* was among them.

For action in Vietnam, the ship received a commendation for "exceptional

Former employees of the now-closed Philadelphia Naval Shipyard continued to get together every now and then to reminisce about their experiences on the *USS New Jersey*. Among the men at O'Donnell's Restaurant in Gloucester City in 1999, are (from left, front table) Sam Trambo, Jim Devlin, Tony Leone, Jack Cleaver, John Borek and Joseph Lampfield.

AVI STEINHARDT, *Courier-Post*

The *USS New Jersey* sits in Dry Dock No. 4, under overhaul at the Philadelphia Naval Shipyard in 1968. The dock was 980 feet long, 130 feet wide and 42 feet deep. It could dock ships as large as Midway (CV41) Class aircraft carriers.
Courtesy of the United States Naval Institute

"I remember like it was yesterday seeing her. I moved equipment out of the engine rooms and marveled at the thickness of the steel in its hull and superstructure."

– Jack Cleaver,
Philadelphia Naval
Shipyard worker

meritorious service" and was awarded three battle stars. Decommissioning was at Puget Sound Naval Shipyard in Bremerton, Washington, on December 17, 1969.

"It was my dream to serve on the *New Jersey* and I was overjoyed when that first dream came true in May 1969," said retired Navy Cmdr. Paul Stillwell, a historian at the U.S. Naval Institute in Annapolis, Maryland, and author of the book, *Battleship New Jersey: An Illustrated History.*

"I love that ship. I remember the formality, the pageantry and the dignity," said Stillwell, who served as an assistant combat information center officer in 1969. "We could never understand how it could be decommissioned during Vietnam when the boys over there needed her firepower."

Robert C. Peniston served on the ship in the 1940s as assistant navigator and then returned to be its last captain during the Vietnam era. He took command five days after the deactivation order was issued in August, supervising the task of putting the ship into mothballs. He was deeply disappointed.

Immortalized in print on a wall inside Turret No. 1 are a portion of his parting words, which were:

"Rest well, yet sleep lightly; and hear the call, if sounded again, to provide firepower for freedom.

"She will hear the call and, thanks to her magnificent crew, she is ready."

The *New Jersey* was to hear the call again, but not for more than a decade.

Philadelphia Naval Shipyard workmen prepare a sheet of metal in November 1967, for welding of a new helicopter pad on the fantail of the battleship.
Courtesy of the United States Naval Institute

Crewmen stow 5-inch powder cans after a high-line transfer from another ship in the Atlantic Ocean in May 1968.

National Archives photo, courtesy of the Home Port Alliance

The *USS New Jersey* at sea on September 9, 1968 (far left). The ship still retains her World War II crane. Clearly visible is the recently installed helicopter flight deck.

Courier-Post archives

The front page of the January 31, 1968, edition of the *Courier-Post* reports the battles that rage in Saigon, Vietnam. It was the second day of the Tet offensive.

Courier-Post archives

Upon completion of service in Vietnam, the *USS New Jersey* enters San Francisco Bay on June 24, 1969, crossing under the Bay Bridge.

National Archives photo, courtesy of the Home Port Alliance

The *USS New Jersey* was in Vietnam to support the Army and Marine ground troops with firepower. Ronald Dash of Willingboro, New Jersey (right, as he presents Willingboro's first war memorial in November 2000) was one of those Marines. "When we were heavily attacked, the New Jersey came in with her fire support and saved us and we will never forget it," Dash said.

JOHN ZIOMEK, *Courier-Post*

The watery impact of 16-inch rounds from the battleship can be seen in this photo taken during gunnery practice in 1968.

Courtesy of the United States Naval Institute

"When we were heavily attacked, the New Jersey came in with her fire support and saved us, and we will never forget it."

– Ronald Dash, Vietnam veteran

A 16-inch projectile, like the ones used aboard the *USS New Jersey*, is shown in comparison to a Volkswagen Beetle. The armor-piercing projectile weighs 2,600 pounds; the car, approximately 1,500 pounds. The 16-inch guns of the *New Jersey* could propel the 6-foot-tall explosive a distance of almost 25 miles, or theoretically, toss the car with five passengers nearly 25 miles.

Courtesy of the United States Naval Institute

"Nobody likes to see the battleships go away, because they are such an awesome statement of U.S. commitment, resolve and power wherever you send them."

– Capt. Ronald Tucker, ship's last captain

BIG GUNS AND MISSILES: A SYMBOL OF AMERICAN MIGHT IS REBORN

December 1982 – February 1991

Instead of dooming the battleship, the advent of new missile technology saved its life.

Looking for a way to resurrect World War II-vintage warships, the Reagan administration proposed modernizing the *Iowa*-class battleships with missile batteries and sending them back to sea. Congress went along, providing $421 million in 1981 for the modernization of the *New Jersey* at Long Beach Naval Shipyard in California.

The *USS New Jersey* was about to enter its fourth and last phase of active duty.

Its new arsenal would include 32 long-range Tomahawk cruise missiles, 16 anti-ship Harpoon missiles and four Vulcan/Phalanx close-in weapons systems for self-defense against aircraft and missiles. Satellite navigation and advanced communication systems also were added, as four of the original 5-inch gun mounts were removed for the missile installation.

President Ronald Reagan attended the recommissioning at Long Beach on December 28, 1982.

"She's gray. She's had her face lifted, but she's still in the prime of life – the gallant lady *New Jersey*. ... God bless and Godspeed," Reagan said.

At the time, the *USS New Jersey* was the world's only active battleship, though recommissioning of its sister ships followed.

The Big J also became the first warship in the Navy to launch a Tomahawk cruise missile. In a test firing May 10, 1983, a Tomahawk blasted off from the ship's fantail, trailing white smoke.

"It was more a political decision to bring her back than a military one," said Paul Stillwell, the Naval Institute historian.

Reagan supported reactivation of the *New Jersey* to "rebuild national pride and spirit in the wake of what had been a nadir in the nation's foreign policy," Stillwell said.

In September 1983, the ship was on a training mission when it was ordered to the Mediterranean Sea. U.S. Marines had gone into Lebanon as part of a multinational peace-keeping force in support of Lebanese forces during Middle East unrest. Syrians

With a rainbow in the background, the *USS New Jersey* enters Subic Bay off Luzon Island in the Philippines during the ship's deployment in southwest Asia.

National Archives photo, courtesy of the Home Port Alliance

President Reagan inspects a Marine detachment before boarding the *USS New Jersey* for the battleship's recommissioning ceremony on December 28, 1982, at the Long Beach Naval Shipyard in California.

National Archives photo, courtesy of the Home Port Alliance

The recommissioning ceremony of the battleship was held at the Long Beach Naval Shipyard in California on December 28, 1982. Standing at the speaker's platform next to the ship's name are (from left) President Reagan; the commanding officer, Capt. William M. Fogarty; the chief of naval operations, Adm. James D. Watkins; and Navy Secretary John F. Lehman Jr. Crewmen of the *New Jersey* man the rail on the bridge and main deck.

National Archives photo, courtesy of the Home Port Alliance

were in mountain positions firing on Marines despite a cease-fire.

The ship played a limited role in keeping Syrian forces in check, mostly as an intimidating presence. The ship would eventually unleash its guns on Syrian forces in Lebanon – but not until nearly two months after the October 23 terrorist bombing of the U.S. Marine barracks at Beirut International Airport, which killed 241 Marines and sailors.

The ship lost a crewman in that bombing – Michael Gorchinski of Lemon Grove, California, who also had spent part of his youth in southern New Jersey, where his father lived. Gorchinski had been dispatched from the ship to the Marine base to assist in the repair of radar equipment. A helicopter from the ship was to pick up the sailor when the bombing occurred.

The *New Jersey's* 16-inch guns fired 11 rounds at Syrian anti-aircraft sites on December 14, 1983, marking the first firing of the ship's guns in combat since the Vietnam War.

"It was meant to send a message to them," said retired Rear Adm. Richard Milligan, the ship's captain at the time.

The battleship's 1,500-member crew and 300 Marines from Beirut were entertained on Christmas Eve 1983 by Bob Hope, Ann Jillian, Brooke Shields and other stars.

The *New Jersey* used its 5-inch guns for a second time in January 1984. And then on February 8, the Big J was allowed to open up with its 16-inch guns. The news brought cheers from the impatient crew. The ship unleashed a 288-round bombardment in the mountains east of Beirut all day and into the night as cover for the Marines; President Reagan had decided to withdraw

"She's gray. She's had her face lifted, but she's still in the prime of life – the gallant lady New Jersey. I hereby place the United States Ship New Jersey in commission. God bless and Godspeed."

– President Ronald Reagan,
at recommissioning

The *USS New Jersey* on sea trials near Long Beach, Calif., on September 25, 1982.
National Archives photo, courtesy of the Home Port Alliance

The *USS New Jersey* fires a broadside at Lebanon as part of its bombardment on February 8, 1984. The ship played a limited role in keeping Syrian forces in check, mostly as an intimidating presence because of internal Navy disputes over naval versus air power. The *New Jersey's* 16-inch guns fired 11 rounds at Syrian anti-aircraft sites on December 14, 1983, marking the first firing of the ship's guns in combat since the Vietnam War.

Courtesy of the United States Naval Institute

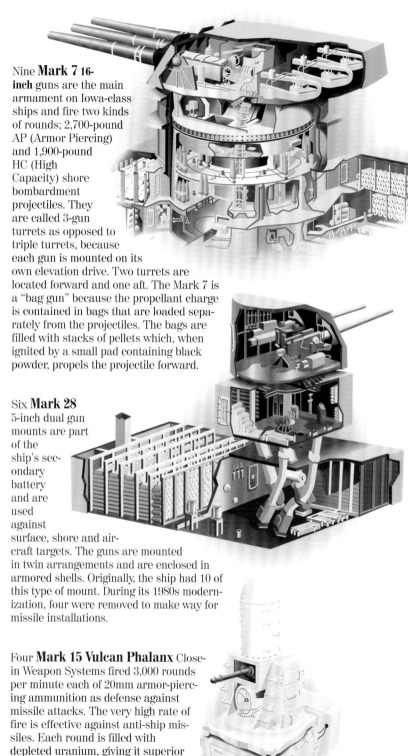

Nine **Mark 7 16-inch** guns are the main armament on Iowa-class ships and fire two kinds of rounds; 2,700-pound AP (Armor Piercing) and 1,900-pound HC (High Capacity) shore bombardment projectiles. They are called 3-gun turrets as opposed to triple turrets, because each gun is mounted on its own elevation drive. Two turrets are located forward and one aft. The Mark 7 is a "bag gun" because the propellant charge is contained in bags that are loaded separately from the projectiles. The bags are filled with stacks of pellets which, when ignited by a small pad containing black powder, propels the projectile forward.

Six **Mark 28** 5-inch dual gun mounts are part of the ship's secondary battery and are used against surface, shore and aircraft targets. The guns are mounted in twin arrangements and are enclosed in armored shells. Originally, the ship had 10 of this type of mount. During its 1980s modernization, four were removed to make way for missile installations.

Four **Mark 15 Vulcan Phalanx** Close-in Weapon Systems fired 3,000 rounds per minute each of 20mm armor-piercing ammunition as defense against missile attacks. The very high rate of fire is effective against anti-ship missiles. Each round is filled with depleted uranium, giving it superior armor-piercing capability.

SHELDON SNEED, *Courier-Post*

A Harpoon anti-ship missile is fired from the *USS New Jersey*. The Harpoon missile was first deployed in 1985, and is capable of being launched from surface ships, submarines or, without the booster, from aircraft. Its over-the-horizon range is 75 to 80 nautical miles.

National Archives photo, courtesy of the Home Port Alliance

most of the Marines and assign them to ships.

It was unclear what damage may have been done because of poor visibility, but Syrian forces did not fire again for more than a week.

"She may not have hit all the targets, but she did what it was intended to do – scare the living daylights out of them," said retired Vice Adm. Douglas Katz of Annapolis, Maryland, a later commanding officer of the ship.

The lieutenant in charge of Turret No. 2 at the time of the Beirut crisis was Robert Lian of Westampton, New Jersey. He said there were internal Navy disputes over whether to use the ship's guns or to continue relying on airstrikes. "I realized the dangers of the job because of the potential for explosions

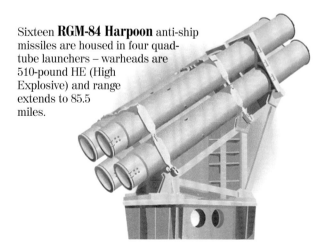

Sixteen **RGM-84 Harpoon** anti-ship missiles are housed in four quad-tube launchers – warheads are 510-pound HE (High Explosive) and range extends to 85.5 miles.

SHELDON SNEED, *Courier-Post*

A starboard quarterview of the battleship (left) is shown during sea trials in September 1982, in the Pacific Ocean off California.

National Archives photo, courtesy of the Home Port Alliance

A Tomahawk long-range cruise missile is fired from the *USS New Jersey*. The missiles are designed to fly at extremely low altitudes at high subsonic speeds. The *New Jersey* was the first to test-fire the Tomahawk.

National Archives photo, courtesy of the Home Port Alliance

Thirty-two **BGM-109 Tomahawk** cruise missiles are housed in eight box launchers that contain four missiles each. The warheads range from 1,000-pound or 980-pound conventional explosive to 293-pound nuclear, and ranges are 470, 675 and 1,500 miles.

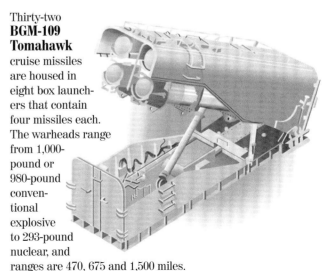

SHELDON SNEED, *Courier-Post*

Crewmen line up to transport case ammunition containers to below-deck magazines during armament replenishment.
National Archives photo, courtesy of the Home Port Alliance

A *USS New Jersey* signalman, dressed in foul-weather gear, uses semaphore to transmit tactical information to other ships in the task group. Arm positions represent letters of the alphabet.
National Archives photo, courtesy of the Home Port Alliance

inside a turret, but I loved this job because it was the closest thing to having command of a ship," Lian said. "It was a challenge to make the guns operate accurately and safely."

When the mission was completed, the *New Jersey* received one more campaign star, boosting its total to 17 since 1943.

With the Navy continuing to focus on aircraft carriers and air power, the role of battleships grew increasingly limited. The *New Jersey's* later missions included naval sea exercises in the Aleutians and appearances off the Korean coast during the 1988 Olympics in Seoul. In 1989, members of its crew boarded the civilian freighter *Ocean Campaigner* after it caught fire and flooded, helping prevent its sinking.

It also became the first U.S. battleship to enter the strategic Straits of Hormuz (separating the Gulf of Oman from the Persian Gulf) and sail deep into the Persian Gulf following the cease-fire in the Iran-Iraq war. For its role in that region, the Navy awarded it two more campaign stars, raising its final count to 19.

The ship then recorded another first before it

was mothballed for the final time in Bremerton, Washington. It became the first battleship to traverse the narrow Columbia River to Portland, Oregon, more than 100 miles from the Pacific Ocean. It went there for a port visit to be showcased at the annual Portland Rose Festival.

Throngs turned out to watch the ship sail up the river, and 40,000 people came aboard for tours during the four-day stop in Portland. It was also greeted by some Greenpeace demonstrators hanging from bungee

The *USS New Jersey* fires its guns (right) in Beirut in the early 1980s.
National Archives photo, courtesy of the Home Port Alliance

The bomb attack that killed U.S. servicemen in Beirut, Lebanon, made headlines around the world. The front page of the October 24, 1983, edition of the *Courier-Post* reported the bloodshed in Beirut, with an early estimate of the number of casualties.

Courier-Post archives

A boatswain's mate operates the controls of a fuel delivery system as a helicopter is refueled on the stern of the *USS New Jersey* while it was in the Pacific Ocean in 1987.

National Archives photo, courtesy of the Home Port Alliance

cords off the Longview Bridge as the ship passed under them.

Capt. Ronald Tucker, the ship's last commanding officer and later a rear admiral, received word in 1990 that his ship was to be deactivated by the following year.

"Nobody likes to see the battleships go away, because they are such an awesome statement of U.S. commitment, resolve and power wherever you send them ... and they make the hearts of old battleship guys go faster," Tucker said.

The Marines loved them, too, he said, but that wasn't enough to justify keeping them afloat.

"God bless the Marines," Tucker said. "They like naval gun fire and I can understand why. There is nothing out there today that from a Marine point of view could possibly replace a 16-inch gun. But the cost of maintaining that capability and all it takes to provide it is not cost-effective."

What was to be the *New Jersey's* last decommissioning came February 8, 1991, at Long Beach Naval Shipyard. As the number of Navy ships dwindled, the *New Jersey* would remain in the reserve fleet for another nine years.

The replenishment oiler *USS Kansas City* (center in photo at right) refuels the *USS New Jersey* (top) and the guided missile destroyer *USS Buchanan,* in the Pacific Ocean on August 12, 1983.

National Archives photo, courtesy of the Home Port Alliance

A sailor on the *USS New Jersey* gets a welcome home hug in 1987.
National Archives photo, courtesy of the Home Port Alliance

The *USS New Jersey* passes the aircraft carrier *USS Midway* in the Pacific Ocean on July 7, 1990 (in photo at left). On the flight deck of the *Midway* are (from right) two F-4 Phantom IIs from Fighter Squadron 151 and an A-6E Intruder.
National Archives photo, courtesy of the Home Port Alliance

A Phalanx gun is fired from the *USS New Jersey*. The Phalanx is a fast-reaction, rapid-fire 20mm gun system that provides ships with a "last-chance" defense against anti-ship missiles and shore-based warfare threats that have penetrated other fleet defenses.
National Archives photo, courtesy of the Home Port Alliance

Crewmen wash down the anchor chain of the battleship. A wash down is required each time the anchor is hoisted.
National Archives photo, courtesy of the Home Port Alliance

"*Rest well, yet sleep lightly; and hear the call, if sounded again, to provide fire-power for freedom. She will hear the call and, thanks to her magnificent crew, she is ready.*"

– Capt. Robert C. Peniston,
in his decommissioning speech,
December 17, 1969

Entering port, *New Jersey* sailors and Marines man the rails.
National Archives photo, courtesy of the Home Port Alliance

The *USS New Jersey* passes the USS Arizona Memorial in Pearl Harbor, Hawaii, on May 24, 1986. Sailors man the rails and the guns are raised in salute to the *Arizona*.
Courtesy of the United States Naval Institute

"She's finally coming back to New Jersey, where we are going to share her with the rest of the world."

– Erwin Sladewski, original crewman

A 24-YEAR QUEST, A JOYFUL RETURN

January 1998 – December 1999

The bid to bring the Big J back to New Jersey began years before it was available as a floating museum.

In 1975, the nonprofit Battleship New Jersey Museum Society was formed to promote the ship's return home. The ship had been sitting in mothballs in Washington state since concluding its Vietnam service in 1969, and would remain there 12 more years before being reactivated one final time. The central Jersey group raised the idea of having the *New Jersey* permanently moored as a tourist attraction at Sandy Hook Bay near the mouth of New York Harbor. In preparation for that day, the group began collecting ship memorabilia.

Two society members, president Victor Dahn of Sea Bright, New Jersey, and Thomas Gorman of Lincroft, New Jersey, raised the profile of the effort when they organized a kick-off rally in Asbury Park on March 14, 1976. The event coincided with Battleship New Jersey Week, which was proclaimed by Gov. Brendan Byrne.

The mighty *USS New Jersey* came up the Delaware River on November 11, 1999, and crowds lined the shores to see its arrival. Hundreds gathered at the Red Bank Battlefield in National Park, New Jersey, to get a glimpse of the Big J.
PARIS L. GRAY, *Courier-Post*

In 1980, the New Jersey Legislature created the New Jersey Battleship Commission to pursue the ship. Byrne, a Democrat, appointed as its chairman Republican Assemblyman Joseph Azzolina, a food chain mogul who was also a naval reservist. The state would later establish two dedicated sources of money for the project – a memorial license plate and a state income tax checkoff fund.

It was not long after the Battleship Commission was formed, however, that the Reagan administration decided it had other plans for the ship; the effort to turn it into a museum would have to be put on hold until the next decade.

But the delay would, by an odd coincidence of timing, give the chairman of the Battleship Commission an opportunity to be on the ship during the last chapter of its active duty. Azzolina was visiting the ship as a naval reserve captain in September 1983 when the captain received orders to sail to the Mediterranean before the Beirut crisis. When the captain asked Azzolina if he wanted to remain, he eagerly stayed aboard for 210 days of the mission.

"That trip made me even more determined to bring the ship back home," said Azzolina, who became part of the ship's story as well as a key figure in returning it to New Jersey.

In the 1990s, as it grew more certain the ship would not fire its guns again, the Battleship Commission still faced a major obstacle: Only two of the four *Iowa*-class battleships, the *Iowa* and the *Missouri,* were being made available for donation as museums. At the insistence of Congress, the *New Jersey* and *Wisconsin* were being retained as part of the active reserve fleet.

Ultimately, on January 4, 1999, Congress agreed to a switch, adding the *New Jersey* to the list of ships for donation and opting to keep the *Iowa* in reserve. It was a change made at the urging of congressmen from several states, including Republican Rep. James Saxton and Democratic Rep. Robert Andrews, both from the region in southern New Jersey vying to host the ship.

Until 1998, it had long been assumed that the site for the ship would be in one of the most highly visited and recognizable places not only in the state but in the world – New York Harbor. The commission had planned to moor the ship off Liberty State Park in Jersey City on the New Jersey side of the harbor, but was forced to drop the plan because of the expense of removing river bedrock.

The commission shifted its focus to a site in Bayonne several miles south of the Statue of Liberty in a more commercial port area of the harbor at the former

In 1980, the New Jersey Legislature created the New Jersey Battleship Commission to pursue the return of the *USS New Jersey.* State Assemblyman Joseph Azzolina (in front of the battleship when it was in Bremerton, Washington), a Republican from Monmouth County who was also a naval reservist, was appointed as its chairman.

CHRIS LACHALL, Gannett N.J. State Bureau/*Courier-Post*

Military Ocean Marine Terminal, an abandoned military installation.

But then, in 1998, the commission heard a renewed plea from South Jersey supporters, who wanted the panel to select Camden, just across the Delaware River from Philadelphia. Camden backers had asked the commission to consider the city years earlier, but the site and several others in South Jersey were dismissed after a cursory review.

The backers of the South Jersey option were part of a bipartisan coalition of political, government, business and labor leaders who called their group the Home Port Alliance. To help their cause, they came up with a catchy slogan: "From Birthplace to Berthplace," which referred to the ship's construction on the Delaware River and its hope-

"A complete, thorough, unbiased look at all sites will lead the Navy to decide the Camden waterfront, near where the USS New Jersey was built by the men and women of the Delaware Valley, is the best place for the final assignment."

– *Courier-Post* editorial

Retired Navy Capt. David McGuigan (left) and retired Rear Adm. Thomas Seigenthaler, both of Haddonfield, New Jersey, led the Home Port Alliance in its fight to have the battleship make its final home on the Camden waterfront. In the early 1980s, Seigenthaler was commander of the Philadelphia Naval Shipyard, where the *USS New Jersey* was built.

AVI STEINHARDT, *Courier-Post*

To express South Jersey's enthusiasm for the *USS New Jersey*, supporters put up signs such as this one, at the Beckett Street Terminal in Camden.
AL SCHELL, *Courier-Post*

ful return to the river as a museum.

The Home Port Alliance believed its site made more sense historically because the ship was built on the Delaware River. It also touted other advantages: The Delaware River's freshwater would be less corrosive to the ship's hull than New York Harbor's saltwater, and Philadelphia offered a great naval tradition as the birthplace of both the Navy and the Marines.

The Battleship Commission, however, would go on to recommend to the Navy in September 1998 that Bayonne be awarded the ship because it was in the most heavily populated part of the state. Spearheading its application was one of its members, retired Rear Adm. George Reider.

Undaunted, the Alliance decided to submit an independent application to the Navy, defining even more sharply the battle lines between South Jersey and the more politically powerful North Jersey. South Jerseyans and Philadelphians rallied around the effort, with South Jersey congressmen getting support from colleagues from Pennsylvania, Delaware, Maryland and New York.

"We believe Camden is the right location and we believe the Navy is likely to agree. We're staying the course and will not be discouraged or turned away," declared Patricia Jones, a Democratic freeholder from Camden County.

Another South Jersey leader fighting to get the ship awarded to Camden was state Sen. John Matheussen of Washington Township. He applauded the work of the Battleship Commission but added: "I cannot stand by and see this ship berthed in North Jersey when it belongs in South Jersey as the centerpiece of a waterfront."

The Camden County government went on to sue the commission, claiming its Bayonne decision was made without adequate analysis. The lawsuit was quickly dropped, however, because Home Port Alliance leaders feared it would jeopardize the group's future application to the Navy.

To lead the Alliance, two Navy men were brought on board as volunteers. Retired Rear Adm. Thomas Seigenthaler of Haddonfield, New Jersey, was named executive director. Retired Navy Capt. David McGuigan, also of Haddonfield, managed the application process.

The *USS New Jersey* is docked at Puget Sound Navy Shipyard in Bremerton, Washington, where it was mothballed in the early 1990s.
National Archives photo, courtesy of the Home Port Alliance

McGuigan became the Alliance's board president, spending more than 1,000 hours along with other volunteers, including board trustees Ann DuVall and Linda Hayes, putting together a 1,700-page application that would wow the Navy.

A Vietnam veteran, McGuigan was a naval architect and engineer who once headed the Naval Ship Systems Engineering Station in Philadelphia. He saw the battleship not only as an important memorial but also as a strong educational tool and tourist attraction that would help Camden and invigorate the naval presence in the region.

Local agencies gave even more credibility to the application by pledging millions of dollars to the project. The Camden Empowerment Zone Corp., a development agency funded with federal dollars, promised the first $1 million at the urging of member Frank Fulbrook. A pledge of $3.2 million followed from the Camden County government.

South Jersey's major newspaper, the *Courier-Post* of Cherry Hill, also championed the cause of the Home Port Alliance, producing nearly 50 editorials in support of the bid to berth the ship in Camden.

"A complete, thorough, unbiased look at all sites," the newspaper said in one of its editorials, "will lead the Navy to decide the Camden waterfront, near where the *USS New Jersey* was built by the men and women of the Delaware Valley, is the best place for the final assignment."

The newspaper also documented each development in the battle, turning out more than 100 stories before the Navy made its final decision.

The Alliance got an unexpected boost from the operators of the Intrepid Air and Space Museum in Manhattan, which features the World War II aircraft carrier *Intrepid*. The museum said it would not make sense economically to have two warships competing for tourists on New York Harbor.

And finally, New Jersey's governor at the time, Republican Christie Whitman, made a decision that would level the playing field for South Jersey. Though previously a supporter of the commission's plan, she took a neutral stance once competition for the ship developed and promised $6 million in state money for restoration would go to whichever group won Navy approval.

On September 11, 1999, the *USS New Jersey* embarked on its final journey to New Jersey. At right, the battleship clears Rich Passage outside Bremerton, Washington. Above, Hugh Dixon, a battleship veteran from Miami, Florida, rises from his wheelchair to pay respects to the ship, as his friend George Chesnut of Redmond, Washington, helps him during the farewell ceremony at Puget Sound Naval Shipyard in Bremerton.

CHRIS LACHALL, Gannett N.J. State Bureau/*Courier-Post*

Workers aboard the *USS New Jersey* prepare the ship for a 5,800-mile tow on September 12, 1999, a day after it left the Puget Sound Naval Shipyard in Bremerton, Washington.

CHRIS LACHALL, Gannett N.J. State Bureau/*Courier-Post*

Robert E. Ingle, Trenton bureau chief for Gannett New Jersey newspapers, covered the battleship's departure from Bremerton, Washington, and its transit through the Panama Canal. In his earlier role as the *Courier-Post's* editorial page editor, Ingle was an early, forceful advocate for locating the ship in Camden.

CHRIS LACHALL, Gannett N.J. State Bureau/*Courier-Post*

Bernie Moran (left in photo at left) and his son Chip, both of Haddon Township, New Jersey, take a last look at the *USS New Jersey* as it sails through Miraflores Lake on its way to the Pedro Miguel Lock in the Panama Canal on October 19, 1999. The Morans were shipbuilders at the Philadelphia Naval Shipyard, where the battleship was built.

CHRIS LACHALL, Gannett N.J. State Bureau/*Courier-Post*

The *USS New Jersey* clears the Bridge of the Americas, the entrance to the Panama Canal near Balboa, on October 16, 1999.

CHRIS LACHALL, Gannett N.J. State Bureau/*Courier-Post*

Home Port Alliance trustee and Camden County Freeholder Patricia Jones (right) went to Panama to see the battleship pass through the Panama Canal. While there, Jones met up with a longtime friend, Ana Elvira Brewer of Panama City, whom she had not seen in more than 25 years.

CHRIS LACHALL, Gannett N.J. State Bureau/*Courier-Post*

As the battle continued, plans were made to bring the ship from Bremerton, Washington, through the Panama Canal before the United States relinquished canal control to Panama at the end of 1999.

In May 1999, the two applications from the competing New Jersey groups were hand-delivered separately to the Navy, which promised a decision by January 2000. The waiting began.

The last voyage of the *New Jersey* was a sentimental journey that could not wait for a decision on the city where it would forever rest.

As Navy officials weighed competing bids from Bayonne and Camden, visiting the two New Jersey communities, the state was arranging for the ship to make a fall 1999 transit of the Panama Canal.

For almost 10 years the "Old Girl," as many affectionately

New Jersey Gov. Christie Whitman is greeted by Panamanian dock workers as she leaves the *USS New Jersey* on October 18, 1999. Whitman was on the battleship as it passed through the Miraflores Locks of the Panama Canal.
CHRIS LACHALL, Gannett N.J. State Bureau/*Courier-Post*

called the ship, had been sitting in the damp climate at the Puget Sound Naval Shipyard in Bremerton, its exterior rusting, its teak deck warping. Now it was time for the ship to come back East.

On September 11, 1999, a farewell ceremony was held in Bremerton led by dignitaries including retired Army Col. Michael Warner, deputy commissioner of Veterans Affairs for New Jersey, and the Battleship Commission's Azzolina.

Original crew member Erwin Sladewski of Manor, Ohio, chaplain of the USS New Jersey Veterans Inc., blessed the ship. His former shipmate, O'Neil Leonard of Ventress, Louisiana, tossed a ceremonial wreath into the sound.

"This ceremony marks the end of the *New Jersey's* great military career, and acknowledges the beginning of an even greater chapter ... as a memorial to what we've done as a nation and what we need to do as a nation," said Capt. Roy Chapple, chief of staff of the Navy's Pacific Northwest Command.

The state of New Jersey paid more than $2

million to have the ship moved to the Philadelphia side of the Delaware River to await its fate. The canal transit alone cost $300,000.

At Bremerton, tugboats positioned themselves for push-and-pull duty along the *New Jersey*, flanked by the aircraft carriers *Midway* and *Ranger*. The ship, stripped of much of its equipment before decommissioning in 1991, was oddly quiet, its 212,000-horsepower engines silent and its four giant propellers locked in place. Finally, the heavy mooring lines were tossed and the battleship *USS New Jersey* was headed home – not under its own steam but under tow, with only a few line handlers on board for the trip.

It was accompanied by a flotilla of ships as it left Puget Sound.

Sea Victory, a tug owned by Crowley Marine Services of Seattle, had the honor of hauling the ship on its two-month journey. The trip began on Sunday morning, September 12, with the sun rising above the Cascade Mountains and the harbor free of its usual morning mist.

The *USS New Jersey* is pulled by electric locomotives, called mules, through the Miraflores Locks in the Panama Canal on October 18, 1999 (left). The locks raised the ship 85 feet above sea level and the battleship was pulled through the canal by a tug. The "mules" that rode atop the locks on both sides kept the ship centered as it moved along at 4 to 5 mph. Taut cables attached between the ship and mules kept it from bumping the sides of the canal. Canal fenders that cushion the ships had to be removed to give the battleship seven to eight inches to spare on either side of the locks.

CHRIS LACHALL, Gannett N.J. State Bureau/*Courier-Post*

Panamanian dock workers prepare to tie the *USS New Jersey* at piers 14 and 15 outside the Panama Canal entrance at Balboa on October 16, 1999.

CHRIS LACHALL, Gannett N.J. State Bureau/*Courier-Post*

Liz Thomas of Moorestown, New Jersey (from left); Capt. Arcelio Hartley, acting manager of transit operations of the Panama Canal; and Michael Warner of Southampton, New Jersey, deputy commissioner of Veterans Affairs for New Jersey, share a light moment after watching the arrival of the *New Jersey* at piers 14 and 15 on the Panama Canal on October 16, 1999.

CHRIS LACHALL, Gannett N.J. State Bureau/*Courier-Post*

The front page of the November 12, 1999, edition of the *Courier-Post* announces the return of the *USS New Jersey*.

Courier-Post archives

On November 10, 1999, the tug *Sea Victory* tows the *USS New Jersey* from the Atlantic Ocean into Delaware Bay.

CHRIS LACHALL, Gannett N.J. State Bureau/*Courier-Post*

The trip went smoothly until the tug and the battleship encountered near gale-force winds in a Pacific storm on October 15, the night before they arrived in Panama. *Sea Victory's* captain, Kaare Ogaard, said the battleship started moving faster than the tug and came up behind it, almost running into the tug. Abandoning plans to anchor, the captain throttled up the tug engines and spent all night in Panama Bay maneuvering to keep the ship heading into the wind.

On October 16, the tug crossed under the Bridge of the Americas and arrived in Balboa, Panama, where the ship would await its turn to transit the Panama Canal from the Pacific entrance to the Atlantic Ocean.

Gov. Christie Whitman led a delegation of about 300 from New Jersey who welcomed the ship and witnessed the historic canal crossing, which occurred just months before the United States

Alfred Decesari of Franklinville, New Jersey, one of the original crew members of the *USS New Jersey*, waits at the now-closed Philadelphia Naval Shipyard to greet the ship as it arrived on November 11, 1999.
SHAWN SULLIVAN, *Courier-Post*

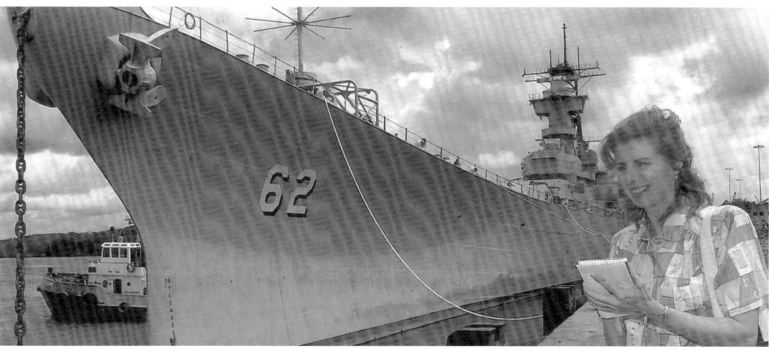

Courier-Post staff writer Carol Comegno was in Panama reporting the *USS New Jersey's* final trip through the Panama Canal en route home to the Delaware River in October 1999. Comegno was on board the Big J for part of its canal journey.
CHRIS LACHALL, Gannett N.J. State Bureau/*Courier-Post*

The *USS New Jersey* makes its way up the Delaware River (left), heading for the former Philadelphia Naval Shipyard, on November 11, 1999.
CHRIS LACHALL, Gannett N.J. State Bureau/*Courier-Post*

Nine-year-old Sean Senavilla of Riverton, New Jersey, watches as the *USS New Jersey* is eased into the dock at the former Philadelphia Naval Shipyard on November 11, 1999.
SHAWN SULLIVAN, *Courier-Post*

A fireboat escorts the *USS New Jersey* as it approaches the former Philadelphia Naval Shipyard on November 11, 1999.

CHRIS LACHALL, Gannett N.J. State Bureau/*Courier-Post*

Thousands of people lined the shores of the Delaware River to get a glimpse of the *USS New Jersey* as it arrived on November 11, 1999. From Soupy Island near National Park, New Jersey, Navy veteran George Anderson (above, from left) and his wife Edna, wait with Suzanne McNulty and her husband, Joe, another Navy veteran, to see the battleship come home.
BOB RINGHAM, *Courier-Post*

George Sinitsky of Mantua, New Jersey (above), commander of Gloucester County Chapter 64, Disabled American Veterans, shows his support for the battleship as it passes by the Red Bank Battlefield in National Park.
PARIS L. GRAY, *Courier-Post*

Boaters on the Delaware River surround the *USS New Jersey* (right photo) as it makes its way up the Delaware toward the former Philadelphia Naval Shipyard.

AL SCHELL, *Courier-Post*

relinquished control of the canal to Panama. Among those who turned out were a dozen former crew members of the ship from all eras, and representatives from the two groups vying for the ship – the Battleship Commission and the Home Port Alliance.

Everyone went aboard the *New Jersey* the day before the trip through the canal, where locks raised the ship 85 feet above sea level. About 75 got the chance to stand on its deck as the battleship was pulled through the canal by a canal tug.

Several locomotive "mules" that rode atop the locks on both sides kept the ship centered as it moved along at 4 to 5 mph. Taut cables attached between the ship and mules kept it from bumping the sides of the canal – at least most of the time. With a beam of slightly over 108 feet at midsection, the *New Jersey* had been designed to fit through the canal. Still, it was tight; canal fenders that cushion the ships had to be removed to give the battleship seven to eight inches to spare on either side of the locks.

The battleship lumbered through the locks smoothly and silently, rising and falling as the locks were closed, filled with water, then emptied, and the gates opened to the next lock. Twice, a puff of smoke and sparks rose from the widest point of its port hull, accompanied by the sound of metal rubbing as the ship brushed against the lock's wall.

Everyone was overwhelmed by the ride.

"I feel exhilarated and consider this my greatest accomplishment," Azzolina said aboard the *New Jersey* as the ship passed through the first canal lock.

"Oh, boy, oh boy, magnificent. Fantastic!" said Joseph Balzano as he stood on the deck. A Home Port Alliance officer and executive director of the South Jersey Port Corp., Balzano would go on to play a key role in the construction of a new pier for the ship.

After crossing Miraflores and Gatun lakes and another set of locks, the *New Jersey* exited the 50-mile canal two days later on October 20, completing its canal crossing in

From aboard the Cape May ferry on November 10, 1999, Harry Ruhle of Collingswood, New Jersey, gets a closer look at the *USS New Jersey* through binoculars, as the battleship passes the ferry in Delaware Bay, a day before its journey upriver to the former Philadelphia Naval Shipyard.

SHAWN SULLIVAN, *Courier-Post*

"The New Jersey is our home state battleship, so it has even more special meaning. It's amazing that in its entire career, only one life was lost in combat."

– Harry Ruhle, Army veteran

Tugs from Moran Towing of Pennsylvania maneuver the battleship and prepare it for berthing at the former Philadelphia Naval Shipyard on November 11, 1999.
CHRIS LACHALL, Gannett N.J. State Bureau/*Courier-Post*

Spectators aboard the tugboat *Jupiter* watch as the *USS New Jersey* is maneuvered into place at the old Philadelphia Naval Shipyard on November 11, 1999. The tug had helped handle the ship at its launching on December 7, 1942.

SHAWN SULLIVAN, *Courier-Post*

From the Twin Capes ferry on the Delaware River, Russell Collins of Palmyra, New Jersey, salutes as the *USS New Jersey* passes by on its way to the former Philadelphia Naval Shipyard on November 11, 1999. Collins served on the battleship during World War II.
RON KARAFIN, *Courier-Post*

On July 27, 2000, the battleship was towed from the old Philadelphia Naval Shipyard to Beckett Street Terminal in Camden. Six-year-old Violet Yantis of Woodbury, New Jersey, watches the battleship from Proprietors Park in Gloucester City, as it heads toward Camden.
AL SCHELL, *Courier-Post*

The mast of the *USS New Jersey* is reflected in the porthole of the tugboat *Suzanne* as the battleship heads toward the Beckett Street Terminal in Camden on July 27, 2000.
PARIS L. GRAY, *Courier-Post*

three days.

Sandor Litai, marine traffic control supervisor for the canal, said the *New Jersey* did well. "We were expecting problems, but they didn't happen," Litai said. "Too bad progress has made her into a dinosaur."

A mechanical problem on board the *Sea Victory* forced another tug to take over the towing temporarily in the Caribbean, but the *New Jersey* still made its destination on time.

November 11 – Veterans Day – was chosen for the final leg up the Delaware River to the former Philadelphia Naval Shipyard, where the ship was built and later modernized. There, the battleship would await the news of its final destination: Camden, just up the river, or Bayonne, a North Jersey community on the west side of New York Harbor.

The *New Jersey's* reception was one befitting a war hero.

Governor Whitman, former crew members and other battleship aficionados – many with tears in their eyes – rode out on a ferry linking Cape May, New Jersey, and Lewes, Delaware, to greet the battleship as it came up the Delaware Bay. More than 25,000 spectators lined the banks of the Delaware River in Delaware, Pennsylvania and New Jersey to watch the ship come in, trailed by recreational boaters. The sound of patriotic music drifted across the river and blasts from antique cannons pierced the air as people of all ages waved flags along the shoreline.

"It gives me the chills," said one of the spectators, Marian Moran of Clementon, New Jersey. Her husband, Bob, had last seen the ship when he took part in the 1945 invasion of Okinawa in World War II.

Terry Schneider, a nurse from National Park, New Jersey, the town almost touched by the ship when it was launched in 1942, held a sign reading: "Welcome Home."

"It was built here and it should stay here," said Schneider, one of the many South

The *USS New Jersey* travels up the Delaware River (above and right), heading for the now-closed Philadelphia Naval Shipyard on November 11, 1999. More than 25,000 spectators lined the banks of the Delaware River in Delaware, Pennsylvania and New Jersey to watch the ship come in, trailed by recreational boaters. Antique cannons were fired, patriotic music played and flags waved as the Big J passed slowly by.

CHRIS LACHALL, Gannett N.J. State Bureau/*Courier-Post*

"It's one of the
most beautiful
sights, with the
sun glowing
on her ....
Rembrandt, eat
your heart out!"

– Jeff Carey, Navy veteran

Among the thousands of spectators who paid tribute to the *USS New Jersey* as it arrived at the former Philadelphia Naval Shipyard on November 11, 1999, was Buck Wooten (left photo), of Baltimore, Maryland, who held up a Welcome Home sign as the battleship passed by. Terri Delliponti of Palmyra, New Jersey (from left in photo above), watches the battleship with two 8-year-olds, Molly Wingert and Lindsay Mills, both of Riverton, New Jersey. Molly and Lindsay were part of a group of third-graders from Riverton who had followed the ship via the Internet, during its trip from Bremerton to Philadelphia.
SHAWN SULLIVAN, *Courier-Post*

Jersey partisans hoping for the city of Camden to win as host city.

Former crewman Robert Walters was so overcome by emotion he couldn't speak when he spotted the ship. "I was thinking of all the buddies of mine who aren't here anymore to see it," he said.

"It's American pride coming up the river," he added. "It's every mother's son who was ever in the service."

Near the old Navy yard, river tugs operated by Moran Towing of Pennsylvania turned the great ship in the middle of the river and eased it stern first alongside a pier at the Navy's Inactive Ships Maintenance Facility, at the former shipyard.

When the ship was safely tucked alongside the pier, the bow was drenched in sunlight and facing its namesake state. South Jerseyans hoped it would not have too much farther to go.

Lindsay Mills, 8, of Riverton, New Jersey, wears a sailor's cap and holds a flag as she watches the *USS New Jersey* as it is eased into the dock at the old Philadelphia Naval Shipyard on November 11, 1999.
SHAWN SULLIVAN, *Courier-Post*

"We tracked her every inch of the way from Washington state to Philadelph-i-a...Great day! The New Jersey's back in town. Great Day! In New Jersey she'll be found."

–Lyrics composed by Riverton, New Jersey, third-graders
and sung to the tune of Erie Canal

Six-year-old Kerri Singley of Voorhees, New Jersey, gets a better view of the *USS New Jersey* from the shoulders of her dad, George, as the battleship is moved into its berth by tugboats.

AL SCHELL, *Courier-Post*

Crowds gather along the banks of the Red Bank Battlefield in National Park, New Jersey, to get a glimpse of the *USS New Jersey* as it heads up the Delaware River toward the now-closed Philadelphia Naval Shipyard on November 11, 1999.
PARIS L. GRAY, *Courier-Post*

The American flag is displayed on the tugboat *Sea Victory* as it pulls out of the former Philadelphia Naval Shipyard (right photo) after delivering the *USS New Jersey* on November 11, 1999. That same day, the tug's master, Capt. Kaare L. Ogaard Jr. (left in photo at left), was presented with a meritorious service medal by maritime artist Jim Flood. Flood represented Rear Adm. Edward Snyder, who was the commanding officer of the *USS New Jersey* during the Vietnam War. Flood also served on the *New Jersey* off Vietnam.
TINA MARKOE KINSLOW, *Courier-Post*

On February 6, 2000, battleship afi-
cionados celebrated the selection of
Camden as the final berth of the *USS
New Jersey*. Lorraine Meehan of
Brooklawn, New Jersey (above),
dances to music by the Two Street
Mummers Band from Philadelphia, at
a party at the E-Centre in Camden.
The entertainment center later
changed its name to Tweeter Center.
Three months earlier, a large crowd
at the Red Bank Battlefield in
National Park, New Jersey, (near
right) welcomed the battleship as it
approached the old Philadelphia
Naval Shipyard on November 11,
1999. Later that day, as the sun set
and the crowds left and the celebra-
tions died down, the mighty battleship sat silently, its bow pointing to
its namesake state.

Photos by CHRIS LACHALL and
SHAWN SULLIVAN, *Courier-Post*

116

"I knew we had the best application, but we're so used to losing, I can't believe we got it!"

– Patricia Jones, Camden County freeholder and Home Port Alliance trustee

COMING FULL CIRCLE: SHIP'S TIES TO REGION PROPEL CAMDEN TO VICTORY

January 2000 – September 2001

On the morning of January 20, 2000, snow fell steadily on the warped and worn deck of the *USS New Jersey* as the hibernating dreadnought rested pierside at the former Philadelphia Naval Shipyard.

A momentous decision was at hand.

Navy Secretary Richard Danzig notified two South Jersey congressmen and the state Battleship Commission that within a few hours, he would announce which New Jersey community had been chosen to host the battleship as a permanent museum.

Republican Rep. James Saxton, Democratic Rep. Robert Andrews and a few members of the Home Port Alliance, the group fighting to win the ship for Camden, hurried over to Philadelphia to take a telephone call from Danzig at the place where the ship was awaiting its fate.

In the meantime, Danzig first notified Gov. Christie Whitman of the Navy's decision: the ship would be going to Camden, across the river from Philadelphia. The Camden site's application had been deemed superior to the one submitted by the Battleship Commission, which sought a final berth in Bayonne near the mouth of New York Harbor.

Danzig described the Camden application as "very strong" – the strongest the Navy had ever received for any ship donation. Most of all,

the Navy said, Camden was chosen because of the established waterfronts in Camden and Philadelphia and the region's historic ties to the ship and the Navy. Community support generated in New Jersey, Pennsylvania and Delaware, and a plan for an on-board Navy recruiting station, also impressed officials in Washington.

"The Navy is very confident that the *New Jersey* will be well cared-for and revered in its new berth on the Delaware River in Camden," Danzig said.

Delaware Valley supporters of the Camden site were jubilant. They had beaten the odds, scoring a victory over a site in the more populated and more politically powerful northern

A jubilant Donald Norcross (left in photo at left), vice president of the Home Port Alliance Board of Trustees and a labor leader, greets Camden County Freeholder Patricia Jones as they hear the news on January 20, 2000, in Philadelphia, that Camden had been selected as the final berth of the *USS New Jersey* (in background). BRIAN PORCO, *Courier-Post*

"She has always been known as a lucky ship. I know her luck will instill - as it did in the thousands who served on her - a spirit of pride and hope ... in a city that has battled against the triple threats of poverty, hopelessness and decay."

– Gov. Christie Whitman,
at welcome-home ceremony, July 28, 2000

A Welcome Home Battleship ceremony is held on the deck of the *USS New Jersey* on July 28, 2000, as it sits at the Beckett Street Terminal in Camden, where the public flocked when the ship opened for a few days before the start of restoration.
PARIS L. GRAY, *Courier-Post*

On January 21, 2000, the *Courier-Post* was proud to announce that the *USS New Jersey* had indeed been awarded to Camden.

Courier-Post archives

part of New Jersey.

"Finally, Camden gets something of value," said Home Port Alliance trustee Patricia Jones, as the group celebrated the announcement. "I knew we had the best application, but we're so used to losing, I can't believe we got it!"

The decision stunned the Battleship Commission, which

had expected its site to win. Assemblyman Joseph Azzolina, the commission's chairman, conceded defeat and sent his congratulations to the Home Port Alliance. Still, the decision did not sit well with the commission, and it weighed a possible legal challenge. Governor Whitman, however, quashed the effort, declaring that the ship "was going to do just fine in Camden."

Jones said perseverance and public support were the keys to success, but she cited retired Navy Capt. David McGuigan as the person most responsible for the successful Camden bid. "Without his writing expertise, ideas and meticulous and tireless work on the application, this wouldn't have happened," she said as her group celebrated alongside the ship in the snowstorm.

"The greatest Navy ship has come full circle – from birth to berth!" declared Sen. John Matheussen, another member of the Alliance.

Joseph Balzano, the Home Port Alliance's board secretary, had dreamed of bringing a tourist ship to Camden for decades but never thought it would be the prestigious battleship. "On a cold, miserable snowy day like this, we get the win of a century," he said. "This is the most successful thing that has happened in my life."

Saxton, as a senior member of the House Armed Services Committee, said the competition had been tough. "I have no doubt the Navy worked hard to pick the best site," he said. "The Camden site simply had incontrovertible advantages over Bayonne and the ship will be crowned the First Lady of the historic Delaware River."

Andrews and the Alliance's board vice president, South Jersey AFL-CIO President Donald Norcross, called it a proud day for South Jersey – especially for those who had served on the ship and those who had built it.

Work on transforming the Big J into a museum could not begin, however, until the ship was moved across the Delaware River to New Jersey. The nonprofit Alliance needed months to work out an agreement turning the ship over to the group. The contract requires the Alliance to file maintenance and financial reports to the Navy, which reserves the option to reclaim the ship in a defense emergency. The Alliance also had to reach an accord with the U.S. Environmental Protection Agency on environmental hazards that might have to be removed or remediated.

Finally, on July 27, the ship was towed three miles up the Delaware River to the South Jersey Port Corp.'s Beckett Street Terminal in Camden, the first of two temporary berths in the battleship's new home. Over two days, an estimated 11,000 visitors took advantage of an offer to get a sneak peek of the ship and walk the main deck.

"She has always been known as a lucky ship," said Gov. Christie Whitman at a welcome-home ceremony July 28. "I know her luck will instill – as it did in the thousands who served on her – a spirit of pride and hope ... in a city that has battled against the triple threats of poverty, hopelessness and decay."

Just a few days later, the *New Jersey* was thrust into the national spotlight when the Republican National Convention got under way in Philadelphia. The ship was showcased on the night of August 1 when retired Gen. Norman Schwarzkopf, a hero of the 1991 Persian Gulf War to free oil-rich Kuwait from Iraq, delivered a nationally televised salute to veterans from aboard the ship.

With several hundred invited veterans in attendance, Schwarzkopf spoke from a brightly lit podium set up on the bow of the ship, with the huge 16-inch gun barrels of the *New Jersey's* No. 1 and No. 2 turrets looming behind him.

"As I stand here on the deck of this great battleship *New Jersey* that made so much history and witnessed so much heroism in its day, surrounded by these proud veterans of American wars in far-flung times and places, I am again reminded of what a great nation we are," Schwarzkopf said.

On August 15, the ship was moved again, this time 1.5 miles down river to a repair yard at South Jersey Port Corp.'s Broadway Marine Terminal – where New York Shipbuilding and Drydock Co. built ships like the carrier *USS Kitty Hawk*.

Now, the effort to bring the Big J back to life could finally begin.

For more than a year, contractors and volunteers worked on the project, targeting a September 2001 opening.

To pay for the restoration, the state and other public agencies contributed additional funds, bringing the amount pledged to more than $22 million.

The Whitman administration funneled the initial $6 million for the work to the Delaware River Port Authority, which it chose to be the oversight agency. The Port Authority, which operates four bridges over the Delaware River while also helping fund waterfront development, offered an additional $2 million as an operating grant. The Home Port Alliance's board, meanwhile, was expanded to include representation from the agencies providing funding.

McGuigan, architect of the Alliance's successful ship application, resigned as the group's pres-

With the *USS New Jersey* as a backdrop, U.S. Reps. Robert Andrews (left) and James Saxton, announced on April 10, 2000, the final plans for the future of the battleship. Both congressmen and U.S. Sen. Robert Torricelli were instrumental in getting Congress to agree to add the *New Jersey* to the list of ships for donation.
TINA MARKOE KINSLOW, *Courier-Post*

John F. Morrow of Turnersville, New Jersey, a former shipyard worker who helped build the *USS New Jersey* in 1942, stands in front of a Welcome to New Jersey sign when it was unveiled on June 15, 2000. The sign, on westbound Route 30 in Camden, features a drawing of the battleship in its center.
RON KARAFIN, *Courier-Post*

May 23, 2001, was the 58th anniversary of the commissioning of the *USS New Jersey*. Rear Adm. Thomas U. Seigenthaler (above, left) and Camden County Surrogate Patricia Jones celebrate with a cake, as Walter E. Olkowski, a member of the New Jersey Battleship Commission, watches.
PARIS L. GRAY, *Courier-Post*

Employees of Eagle Marine Industrial Services in Blackwood, New Jersey, board the *USS New Jersey* at the old Philadelphia Naval Shipyard on July 27, 2000. The workers handled the lines for the battleship's journey from the Philadelphia side of the Delaware River to the Beckett Street Terminal in Camden.

RON KARAFIN, *Courier-Post*

Line runners Paul Myers of Sewell, New Jersey (left), and Harry McCleery of Pitman, New Jersey, release the bow line to the *USS New Jersey* at the former Philadelphia Naval Shipyard on July 27, 2000. It was the start of the ship's journey to the Camden side of the river.

RON KARAFIN, *Courier-Post*

The *USS New Jersey* passes under the Walt Whitman Bridge on July 27, 2000, as it heads to the Beckett Street Terminal.

PARIS L. GRAY, *Courier-Post*

On August 15, 2000, the *USS New Jersey* is moved once again, this time to the Broadway Terminal, where it would undergo partial restoration.

AL SCHELL, *Courier-Post*

The *USS New Jersey* is guided by tugboats from one pier to an adjacent pier at the Broadway Terminal in Camden, while undergoing refurbishment in preparation for its becoming a museum.
CHRIS LACHALL, *Courier-Post*

ident in late 2000, citing personal reasons. Unable to agree on a single leader to replace him, the Alliance appointed two co-chairs: Senator Matheussen, a Republican, and Jones, a Democrat just elected as Camden County surrogate. Jones had been a county freeholder when the battleship was awarded to Camden.

Hundreds of volunteers became involved in the restoration, logging more than 90,000 hours leading up to the museum ship's opening. Former crew members, shipyard workers and others helped clean, paint, fix communications systems, replace missing equipment and log historical artifacts.

"The outpouring has been phenomenal," said Joseph Fillmyer of Cinnaminson, New Jersey, the Alliance's director of volunteers. "People have come from all over the country and the world to volunteer their time."

Engineer Peter Greene and other employees of L3 Communications Systems in Camden, a supplier of Navy communications systems, repaired the disabled internal communications systems and also established a shipboard ham radio club. Edwina Alber of Medford, New Jersey, painted galley tables and a small boat on the ship and later volunteered as a docent. "The ship just becomes part of you and I want to pass on history down to other generations," she said.

Former World War II crew members like Robert LaVine, of Warren, New Jersey, and John Horan, of Cherry Hill, New Jersey, did odd jobs in the areas of the ship where they once ate and slept.

Professional contractors were hired to paint the ship's exterior, perform environmental work and install utilities, including modified air conditioning, heating and sanitary systems, at a cost of nearly $7 million. Hill International of Willingboro, New Jersey, a project management firm, supervised the work.

A concrete and steel T-shaped pier was built at a cost of $11 million, and a $1 million temporary visitor center and ticketing area were constructed ashore for the ship's grand opening.

In an attempt to heal wounds, the Alliance sought to involve the longstanding battleship organizations that had worked so hard to get the ship placed in North Jersey. The Battleship New Jersey Foundation, which raises funds for the Battleship Commission and receives state license plate and income tax checkoff revenue, provided $1.4 million for Combat Engagement Center restoration, mannequins for ship exhibits and lights for exterior illumination. The Battleship New Jersey Museum Society was given space on the ship to display historic artifacts it had collected since the 1970s.

"We still have a little war between the north and south, but I think the Navy made the right decision," said Richard Esser, president of USS New Jersey Veterans Inc., a national organization made up of former crewmen of the ship. "The Alliance has done a gorgeous job of fixing up the ship and I've been impressed with all the work the volunteers have done."

Three-year-old Collin Miller of Deptford, New Jersey, holds the flag as he watches the *USS New Jersey* arrive at the Beckett Street Terminal in Camden on July 27, 2000.
PARIS L. GRAY, *Courier-Post*

Restoration work on the Central Communications Center on the main deck of the *USS New Jersey* was under way on December 12, 2000, when the battleship was docked at the Broadway Terminal in Camden.
RON KARAFIN, *Courier-Post*

The weathered main deck of the *USS New Jersey* sprawls before the now-silent guns of Turret No. 1. Behind looms the bridge where naval personnel of all ranks and rates walked through U.S. naval history.
RON KARAFIN, *Courier-Post*

Helmets used for damage-control situations aboard the *USS New Jersey* are stowed atop one another in racks.
RON KARAFIN, *Courier-Post*

Retired Gen. Norman Schwarzkopf (center) arrives before his speech to the Republican National Convention in Philadelphia on August 1, 2000. Schwarzkopf, who was instrumental in the success of Operation Desert Storm, delivered his speech from the *USS New Jersey*.

SCOTT ANDERSON, *Courier-Post*

Tomahawk missile launchers are on the 03 level of the *USS New Jersey*. The Tomahawk missiles made a widely witnessed debut during Operation Desert Storm in 1991.

RON KARAFIN, *Courier-Post*

Inside the *USS New Jersey*, the captain's quarters are on the ship's 01 level. During World War II, this space was used by Admirals Raymond Spruance and William Halsey. In the foreground is the case that normally holds the ship's silver service, which is usually donated by the ship's namesake state.

RON KARAFIN, *Courier-Post*

The Combat Engagement Center of the *USS New Jersey* is silent and minus equipment on December 12, 2000, as the battleship undergoes restoration prior to its opening as a museum.
RON KARAFIN, *Courier-Post*

The Tomahawk firing control panels on the *USS New Jersey* are inside the Combat Engagement Center.
RON KARAFIN, *Courier-Post*

A seal of the Home Port Alliance, the group that was responsible for bringing the *USS New Jersey* to Camden, was on display on the center 16-inch gun of Turret No. 1, on December 12, 2000.
RON KARAFIN, *Courier-Post*

Steep ladders leading to deck passageways of the *USS New Jersey* reflect the compactness of design in the 1940s-era battleship.
RON KARAFIN, *Courier-Post*

The Armored Conning Station inside the bridge of the *USS New Jersey* is an armored compartment that allows personnel to operate the ship in greater safety during battle.
RON KARAFIN, *Courier-Post*

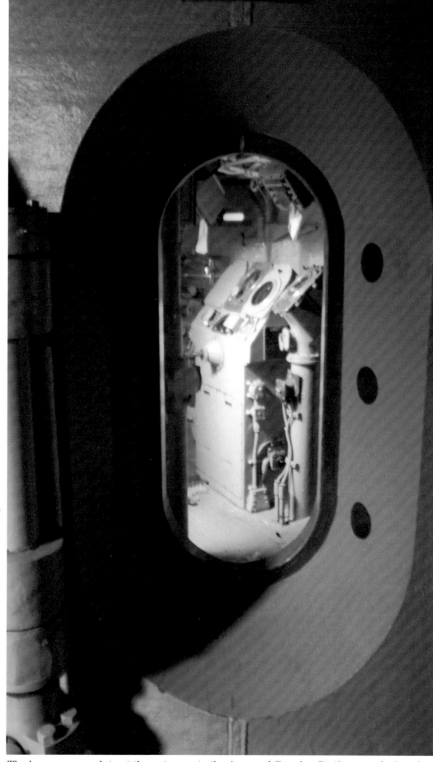

The heavy armor plate at the entrance to the Armored Conning Station was designed to withstand strong blasts during combat.

RON KARAFIN, *Courier-Post*

Turrets No. 1 and No. 2 on the *USS New Jersey* are located forward of the superstructure. Turret No. 3 is aft.
RON KARAFIN, *Courier-Post*

The original insignia of the battleship is painted on one of its interior doors.
RON KARAFIN, *Courier-Post*

The 3rd Division office door on the ship bears this rendering.
RON KARAFIN, *Courier-Post*

While the battleship was mothballed, its stack suffered weathering.
RON KARAFIN, *Courier-Post*

Years of exposure to the humid climate in the Pacific Northwest took its toll on the battleship's walkway (left) and wood deck (right).
RON KARAFIN, *Courier-Post*

Anchor chains can be seen in the foreground when looking aft from the bow on the main deck of the *USS New Jersey*.

RON KARAFIN, *Courier-Post*

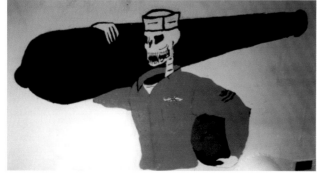

Sailors left their mark on an inside bulkhead of the battleship's Turret No. 1.

RON KARAFIN, *Courier-Post*

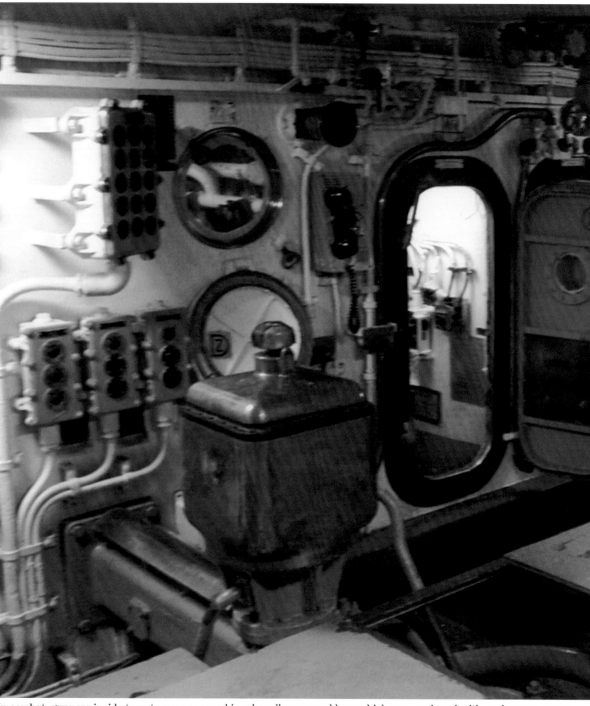

In combat, gunners inside turrets were encased in a heavily armored box, which was equipped with periscopes, range finders, auxiliary computers and communication indicators.

RON KARAFIN, *Courier-Post*

Joseph Fillmyer, of Cinnaminson, New Jersey, director of volunteer programs for the Home Port Alliance, stands near the breech, where 16-inch rounds were inserted for firing.
RON KARAFIN, *Courier-Post*

On a different trip to the ship, Fillmyer looks through a periscope in Turret No. 1.
AL SCHELL, *Courier-Post*

A passageway connecting the engine and boiler rooms on the third deck of the *USS New Jersey* is lined with instruments, flasks and pipes. This passageway early in the history of the *Iowa*-class ships was termed "Broadway."

RON KARAFIN, *Courier-Post*

Inside the boiler room is a heat exchanger, seen in this closeup view.

RON KARAFIN, *Courier-Post*

The battleship stands tall at the Broadway Terminal in Camden on December 12, 2000, as it undergoes restoration. The graceful sheer of the *Iowa*-class ship is clearly visible.

RON KARAFIN, *Courier-Post*

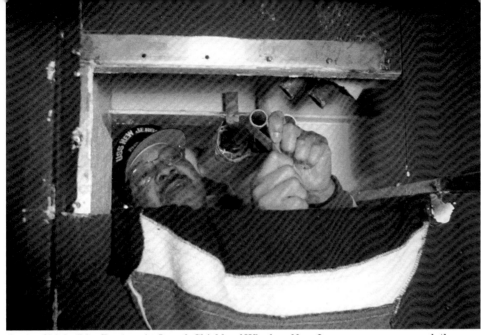

Senior Shipbuilder/Boatswain Joseph Shields of Winslow, New Jersey, uses an emery cloth on piping aboard the *USS New Jersey* during restoration at the Broadway Marine Terminal in Camden.

AVI STEINHARDT / *Courier Post*

Volunteer John Saracen of Mount Holly, New Jersey, works on a general announcing system on the ship on March 17, 2001. The system had been disabled as part of the mothballing process. It is used to transmit not only voice alarms, but also general, chemical, fire, biological and collision alarms.

SHAWN SULLIVAN, *Courier-Post*

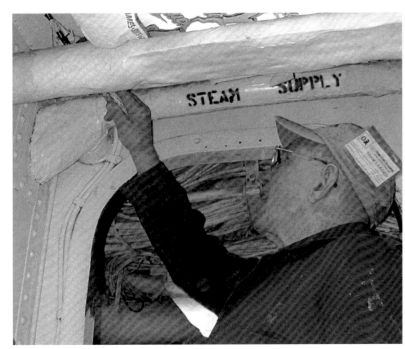

To help in the battleship's restoration, volunteers gave their time and expertise. Above, Frank Larkins of Deptford, New Jersey, scrapes loose paint overhead on March 2, 2001. The 80-year-old was a volunteer team leader.

CLARK PERKS, *Courier-Post*

Shipkeeper Dominador DelRosario of Waterford, New Jersey, works on the *USS New Jersey* on January 4, 2001.

AVI STEINHARDT, *Courier-Post*

Bernardette Menna of Cherry Hill, New Jersey, removes paper from a door after the compartment was painted on March 2, 2001. Menna had been doing volunteer work on the ship since the beginning of the year.

CLARK PERKS, *Courier-Post*

On December 6, 2000, a ceremony marking Pearl Harbor Day was held alongside the *USS New Jersey*. Marty Seroter of American Legion Post #371 in Gibbsboro, New Jersey, plays "Taps" at the ceremony.
AL SCHELL, *Courier-Post*

Tim Williams of Gloucester City, New Jersey, paints the hull of the *USS New Jersey* on August 6, 2001 (left). For more than a year, contractors and volunteers worked on the restoration project. To pay for the restoration, the state and other public agencies contributed funds, bringing the amount pledged for the ship's T-shaped pier and visitor's center to more than $22 million.
SCOTT ANDERSON, *Courier-Post*

On July 25, 2001, work was under way on the pier that would be the final berth of the battleship on the Camden waterfront.
AL SCHELL, *Courier-Post*

When the *USS New Jersey* arrived at the Beckett Street Terminal in Camden on July 27, 2000, George Martella of Bellmawr, New Jersey, a former chief petty officer boatswain, pipes "attention on deck" to those on the pier to welcome the ship. The use of Bo'sn pipes is a longstanding Navy tradition that dates back to sailing ship days.
AL SCHELL, *Courier-Post*

The battleship was the scene of ceremonies that touched several veterans. On December 6, 2000, members of the Marine Corps League fired off a 21-gun salute to the ship at an annual Pearl Harbor Day ceremony, sponsored for the 10th year by U.S. Rep. Robert E. Andrews. The ceremony was held at South Jersey Port Corp.'s Broadway Terminal while the ship was undergoing restoration.
AL SCHELL, *Courier-Post*

On December 7, 1999, the annual Pearl Harbor Day ceremony was held at the former Philadelphia Naval Shipyard, where the battleship had been docked after its transit from Bremerton, Washington. Saluting the ship were (from left) John Cellini of Collingswood, New Jersey, and Mario Musciano of Somerdale, New Jersey. Both were members of the Garden State chapter of the Pearl Harbor Survivors Association.
RON KARAFIN, *Courier-Post*

At the Welcome Home Battleship ceremony on July 28, 2000, Bob Weimann of Woodbury, New Jersey, solemnly honors the ship.
PARIS L. GRAY, *Courier-Post*

A MONUMENT TO FREEDOM

Public opening: October 15, 2001

The Battleship New Jersey Memorial and Museum opened to the public on a crisp, clear fall day in 2001, perfect weather for touring the restored warship. After a 14-month restoration, the ship was ready for visitors, but were visitors ready to tour the ship?

Would the September 11 terrorist attacks against the United States and new threats of terrorism keep people away from the newest tourist attraction on the Camden waterfront?

Or would the renewed sense of patriotism sweeping the country give people added incentive, in the days and months to come, to visit a ship that had come to symbolize America's commitment to freedom?

On October 15, 2001, one day after the ship's grand opening, eight former Marines made up the first group to take a public tour of the floating museum at 62 Battleship Place.

"We should all salute it," said retired Lt. Col. Al Bancroft of Voorhees, New Jersey, a member of that group. "It's great we have a tribute like this, a tribute to all veterans."

Marie Kirk of Marlton, New Jersey, another first-day visitor, was overwhelmed. "I've still got goose bumps," she said. "When you see it standing a distance from it, it's enormous, but once you get on it, it's

even bigger – especially those guns!"

By day's end, 458 people had taken the tour, including former *New Jersey* crew members and 12 servicemen still on active duty. By week's end, the number of visitors had reached 4,405.

Museum Program Director Jack Shaw was both pleased and relieved.

"The tendency against traveling and spending disposable income has been neutralized by a renewed sense of patriotism," Shaw said.

During two-hour guided tours, visitors saw a ship restored to near-working condition in many areas, a mini-city that once bustled with services ranging from a post office, laundry and barbershop to doctor's and dentist's offices and a chapel.

These were some of the scenes tourists could see:

In the Combat Engagement Center, heart of the warship, a white sweep line constantly rotates on

Commemorative battleship envelopes, postmarked from Camden, New Jersey, on October 15, 2001, were available on the opening of the Battleship New Jersey Memorial and Museum.
RON KARAFIN, *Courier-Post*

Swing dancers perform the Lindy and jitterbug at the foot of the pier on October 15, 2001, when the Battleship New Jersey Memorial and Museum opened to the public. Karen Haresign of Mount Laurel, New Jersey, and Eric Heitzman of Philadelphia, members of Center City Swings, a Philadelphia group, boogied to a live radio broadcast of Big Band-era tunes from World War II.
RON KARAFIN, *Courier-Post*

An hour before the *New Jersey* opened for public tours on October 15, 2001, earlybirds show up at the Visitors Center to buy tickets.
RON KARAFIN, *Courier-Post*

a working radar scope. Missile imagery appears on another console, and computer monitors show the red and yellow fireball blasts from the 16-inch guns. In the radio room, telephones ring, a hand-powered phone squawks and the typewriter keys of a news service teletype machine clack. Inside 16-inch gun Turret No. 1, a shell weighing about a ton sits in a cradle ready to be loaded into one of the three gun barrels.

"Great tour. I didn't realize they had so many departments to run this big gal," marveled Air Force veteran Barbara Parker, a first-day visitor from Willingboro, New Jersey.

Visitors to the Big J can enter all the compartments on the tour, unlike other museum ships, where tourists must sometimes peer through plastic glass or stand behind roped-off doorways.

"We wanted to make our experience as lifelike and informative as possible, so we have made the public areas of our ship very accessible," said the ship's curator, Scott Kodger. "This is a unique experience in naval museums."

Mannequins are dressed in authentic uniforms. And docents, or guides, must pass a test before they can lead tours.

On opening day, groups of visitors were greeted by docents in khaki uniforms or blue denim bell-bottoms. They were then escorted to the bow, where they stopped between anchor-handling gear and the 16-inch gun Turret No. 1 in an area known as the forecastle. The docents then led them on a winding route up and down seven decks and steep ladders with little head room, giving them a glimpse into the life of a battleship sailor.

Some visitors passing a wax mannequin of Adm. William Halsey, standing

Invited guests walk up to the *USS New Jersey* on a breezy October 14, 2001, when nearly 1,000 attended the grand opening of the Battleship New Jersey Memorial and Museum.
CHRIS LACHALL, *Courier-Post*

A scale model of the *USS New Jersey*, put on display first at Echelon Mall in Voorhees, New Jersey, in February 2001, was destined to join the exhibits at the Battleship New Jersey Memorial and Museum on the Camden waterfront.

JOSE F. MORENO, *Courier-Post*

Volunteer David DiMarzio, of Pennsville, New Jersey, talks to another volunteer on the other side of a port on the *USS New Jersey* on the opening day of the memorial and museum.

RON KARAFIN, *Courier-Post*

Among the visitors on board the *USS New Jersey* for the first tour of the day on October 15, 2001, are George W. Charlton Jr. (left), sergeant-at-arms of the Marine Corps League, Pfc. Daniel Giordano, Detachment #200 in Somerdale, New Jersey; and retired Lt. Col. Al Bancroft, of the Camden County Clerk's Office.

RON KARAFIN, *Courier-Post*

Heather Warnick of Glassboro, New Jersey, and her 14-month-old son, Jacob, get a look at the 16-inch guns on Turret No. 1 of the *USS New Jersey* on the opening day of the memorial and museum.
RON KARAFIN, *Courier-Post*

With Turret No. 1 in the background, John F. Mills of Maple Shade, docent on the *Battleship New Jersey* (third from right), gives his first tour of the *USS New Jersey* to retired Marines (from left), Lt. Col. Al Bancroft, of the Camden County Clerk's Office; Bobbie Swain of Voorhees, New Jersey, of the Department of New Jersey Marine Corps League; George W. Charlton Jr., sergeant-at-arms of the Marine Corps League, Pfc. Daniel Giordano Detachment #200 in Somerdale, New Jersey; Richard T. Hart of Stratford, New Jersey, paymaster of the Marine Corps League, Pfc. Daniel Giordano Detachment #200; John T. Mason and Donald F. Burkhard, both of Pitman, New Jersey; and members of the Marine Corps League Semper Fidelis Detachment in Wenonah, New Jersey.

RON KARAFIN, *Courier-Post*

"Great tour. I didn't realize they had so many departments to run this big gal."

– Air Force veteran Barbara Parker

Invited guests walk up the pier on their way to the *USS New Jersey* during the ship's grand opening as a memorial and museum.

CHRIS LaCHALL, *Courier-Post*

John F. Mills of Maple Shade, New Jersey, a docent on the *New Jersey*, shows a group of retired Marines where a magnetic compass was located on the center line of the ship.
RON KARAFIN, *Courier-Post*

In the fireroom of the battleship, Jerome Marr of San Jose, California (left), tells Scott Kodger, director of curatorial affairs on the Battleship *New Jersey* (kneeling), and Steven Cox of Detroit, Michigan, how he and his men used to light the boiler when he was serving on the *USS New Jersey* as the boiler officer from 1988 to 1990. Cox also served on the *New Jersey*, but earlier in the 1980s.
RON KARAFIN, *Courier-Post*

"I think they've done an incredible job of repairing the ship and keeping it in good condition – even better than when I was on it."

– Jerome Marr,
a boiler officer from 1988 to 1990

with his binoculars on the Flag Bridge, were startled at the resemblance to the man most had only seen in pictures.

Visitors climbed inside gun turrets and walked into berthing areas where sailors bunked four high. They also saw the captain's cabin, navigation bridge and the box launchers that fired Tomahawk cruise missiles.

Docents staffed several stations,

including the Combat Engagement Center and radio room. They explained how Morse Code was used to send messages, and how the *New Jersey* tracked enemy ships as well as the path of its missiles.

At the "gedunk," or ice cream, stand, visitors could buy snacks just as sailors once did.

The docents rattled off statistics to their tour groups: Each of two bow anchor

chains weigh 30,000 pounds, and each are 1,100 feet long; the boilers used to generate 212,000 shaft horsepower for the four steam turbine engines and steam for other equipment and electricity; the 16-inch guns could fire a shell almost 25 miles.

One docent, Bernardette Menna of Cherry Hill, New Jersey, started work on the ship in January 2001, taping and papering the ship to prepare it for painting.

Paul Hanson of Aston, Pennsylvania, a docent on the *New Jersey* (right), conducts a tour of the ship's Combat Engagement Center under special lighting on the opening day of the memorial and museum.

RON KARAFIN, *Courier-Post*

Jan Supco, an artist with the Quinlen Scenic Studio in Marcus Hook, Pennsylvania, puts the finishing touches to a mural inside the *USS New Jersey* on October 20, 2001.
PARIS L. GRAY, *Courier-Post*

After touring the *USS New Jersey*, Marie and Jesse Kirk of Marlton, New Jersey (right), buy pins and other souvenirs in the battleship's gift shop in the visitors center.
RON KARAFIN, *Courier-Post*

ing it a few tenths of a knot more speed.

"I think they've done an incredible job of repairing the ship and keeping it in good condition – even better than when I was on it," Marr said.

He demonstrated to the staff, ever eager to document how the ship was operated, how the boilers were fired by ramming a flaming rag into an igniter port.

Kodger said the spaces along "Broadway," the uninterrupted passageway connecting the engine and boiler rooms, would be made part of future tours. The Alliance also planned to offer shorter tours, including one covering only the main deck and video tours for people who can't get around.

Thomas Seigenthaler, the Alliance's executive director, said the museum was a work in progress and would be for a long time. Not completed at the time of the opening were elevators to help people with disabilities. The 200-foot walkway to the pier also still needed to be bricked, and it awaited lights and benches.

The staff also was seeking to secure a helicopter for the ship's fantail, 20mm and 40mm gun mounts and some of the ship's silver service, housed at the New Jersey governor's mansion at Drumthwacket.

At its opening, the ship had about 100 docents, all volunteers except for the supervisors. The goal was to expand the work force to at least 200.

The docents, ship crew and other staff included veterans from different branches of the military, former crewmen of the *New Jersey* and other Navy warships, and former shipbuilders from the region. They were able to weave their own sea yarns into the information they provided visitors, making the tours even more memorable.

The museum set a target of 250,000 to 300,000 visitors a year to help meet the projected $5 million operating budget – about the same annual cost as the battleship Missouri operation in Hawaii. Seigenthaler said donations and grants would be sought for future capital improvements.

In January 2002, the New Jersey Legislature approved an additional $7.2 million state grant. Gov. James E. McGreevey asked the Legislature to delete the state grant to help close a $2.9 billion budget deficit. The museum's operators sought the money for improvements, but the Delaware River Port Authority, overseer of state grants to the ship, wanted to use it as partial reimbursement for $6 million it lent to finish the pier.

An Alliance capital fund-raising plan was being developed to finance a museum ashore as well as to

"When you come on board, you fall in love with it," she said. "There was the excitement of getting it ready and now the excitement of telling others about it to preserve it for generations."

Former crewmen were allowed to visit some of the closed areas where they once slept or worked.

Naval Academy graduate Jerome Marr, 38, of San Jose, California, was thrilled when he was taken below to the engineering spaces – not part of a tour route yet – to see the boilers he was in charge of as the boiler officer from 1988 to 1990. The former lieutenant, now an Internet consultant, had been visiting friends in Philadelphia when he found out the *New Jersey* was opening.

He snapped photographs everywhere. Happily discussing his days as a battleship sailor, he recalled setting a record speed of more than 37 knots during sea trials. He said the ship accidentally skimmed the top of a sand bar, scraping off some of its keel barnacles and giv-

A lifelike mannequin of Adm. William Halsey stands on the Flag Bridge of the restored *USS New Jersey*. The battleship was one of Halsey's flagships during World War II in the Pacific Theatre.
SHAWN SULLIVAN, *Courier-Post*

On grand opening day of the *USS New Jersey*, museum docent Paul Viens of Downingtown, Pennsylvania, explains the operation of a 16-inch gun turret. On the right is a mannequin of a turret officer.
CHRIS LACHALL, *Courier-Post*

Al Myers, a foreman at C.M. Company in Atco, New Jersey, removes the nickel plating on the steel bell of the *USS New Jersey* on September 25, 2001.
SHAWN SULLIVAN, *Courier-Post*

Visitors to the *USS New Jersey* can see mannequins in Navy uniforms man the radar and Harpoon missile launch console in the ship's Combat Engagement Center.
SHAWN SULLIVAN, *Courier-Post*

replace the teak deck, sections of which date to World War II or the Vietnam era. The deck replacement alone would cost an estimated $6 million, Seigenthaler said.

To help raise more operating revenue, the Alliance offered ship memberships with special privileges including overnight stays, and sleepovers to groups like the Girl Scouts and Boy Scouts. It also made the ship available for private functions.

To help educate the public about the ship, the state planned to make the history of the *USS New Jersey* a part of the curriculum for elementary and high school students. Kean University in Elizabeth, New Jersey, was developing course material that was expected to be taught by the fall of 2002.

From the ranks of these schoolchildren will have to come the next generation of visitors, volunteers and ship stewards – helping to ensure that a patriot that once provided "firepower for freedom" endures as a monument to freedom.

McGuigan, who as a midshipman polished the Japanese surrender plaque on the Missouri, had youth in mind when he prepared the battleship application for the Alliance.

"If we don't educate our youth to our past history, sacrifices and dedication and to the meaning of service," McGuigan said, "we can't expect them to dedicate themselves and serve in the future – and not just for the battleship but for the nation."

Volunteers who helped support and restore the battleship gather on the main deck of the *USS New Jersey*. The volunteers were at the October 14, 2001, grand opening of the Battleship New Jersey Memorial and Museum.

CHRIS LACHALL, *Courier-Post*

Former and current members of the Home Port Alliance pose for a group photo with the *USS New Jersey* in the background. They are (from left) Jay Jones, retired Navy Capt. David B. McGuigan, Ann DuVall, Frank Fulbrook, Norman Sooy, Philip Norcross, Philip Rowan, Joseph Balzano, Patricia Jones, Sen. John Matheussen and Donald Norcross. Others not pictured are Camden Mayor Gwendolyn Faison, Glenn Paulsen, Andrew Sinclair, Thomas Corcoran, Joan Davis, retired Army Col. Michael Warner and Linda Hayes.

SHAWN SULLIVAN, *Courier-Post*

Heightened security was the result of concern about terrorism. A New Jersey state trooper patrols the ship during the October 14, 2001, grand opening of the Battleship New Jersey Memorial and Museum.

CHRIS LACHALL, *Courier-Post*

Joe Rullo of VFW Post 6332 in Washington Township, New Jersey, salutes during the playing of the national anthem aboard the *USS New Jersey*. Rullo was among veterans from Gloucester County awarded the New Jersey Distinguished Service Award on September 25, 2001.

AVI STEINHARDT, *Courier-Post*

Benjamin Gorchinski of Pleasantville, New Jersey, whose son, Michael, a crew member of the *USS New Jersey*, was killed in the Marine barracks bombing in Beirut, Lebanon, in 1983, attended the grand opening of the Battleship New Jersey Memorial and Museum on October 14, 2001. With Gorchinski is his friend, Jean Madsen of Pleasantville.

CHRIS LaCHALL, *Courier-Post*

Patrolman Ed Haverty of the Camden County Park Police searches Robert Clower of Georgia with a hand-held metal detector as a security precaution during the grand opening of the Battleship New Jersey Memorial and Museum. Clower was wounded when he served on the *USS New Jersey*.

CHRIS LaCHALL, *Courier-Post*

The chaplain who offered a prayer at the *USS New Jersey*'s fourth and final decommissioning in 1991, Capt. James P. Nickols of Williamsburg, Virginia, said the invocation at its rebirth as a museum.

CHRIS LaCHALL, *Courier-Post*

Steve Warnick of Glassboro, New Jersey, lifts his 3½-year-old son, Brett, so the boy could touch a 16-inch gun on Turret No. 1 of the *USS New Jersey* on opening day. The ship's final mission had begun.

WELCOME HOME!

the

camden county Improvement Authority

is proud of its role to help bring home
the Battleship U.S.S. New Jersey

Providing public and private bond financing, economic development, workforce development, and affordable housing for Camden County.

Members
    Fredric B. Weinstein, Chairman
    James B. Kehoe, Vice Chairman
    Joseph P. Schooley
    Terrence M. Carr
    Samuel M. Siler
Philip P. Rowan, Executive Director
Louis R. Meloni, Esq., Solicitor

Freeholder Director Jeffrey L. Nash
Freeholder Deputy Director Edward T. McDonnell

1909 Route 70 East
Suite 300
Cherry Hill NJ 08003
Tel 856.751.CCIA (2242)
Fax 856.751.2247
ccia@co.camden.nj.us